THE
LAWS
OF
FAITH

ONE WORLD BEYOND
DIFFERENCES

What is El Cantare, God of the Earth?

RYUHO OKAWA

IRH PRESS

BOOKS
IRH PRESS
New York

Library of Congress Cataloging-in-Publication Data

ISBN 13: 978-1-942125-34-1
ISBN 10: 1-942125-34-8

Printed in Canada

First Edition

Book Design: Whitney Cookman
Cover Image: © Shutterstock / Atthapol Saita

Contents

CHAPTER ONE
The Power to Believe
Creating a New Reality for Your Life and the World

Life-Changing Words 1:
The Limitless Power of Faith, and the Miracles to Cure Illnesses

CHAPTER TWO
Starting from Love

Solve Life's Problems and Become an Expert in the Study of Life

Life-Changing Words 2:
To Love is to Set Others Free,
Believing the Goodness of Their Hearts

CHAPTER THREE
The Gate to the Future

Use Your 30,000 Days of Life to Benefit the World

Life-Changing Words 3:
Have a Strong Conviction on Wealth

CHAPTER FOUR
The World Religion of Japanese Origin will Save the Earth

Building up a Nation that will Serve to Eliminate All Conflicts from This Planet

Life-Changing Words 4:
Towns with 100 People Who Believe in Me
Shall Not See Catastrophic Natural Disasters

CHAPTER FIVE

What is the Faith in the God of the Earth?

Living in the Age of the New Genesis of Earth

CHAPTER SIX

The Choice of Humankind

Uphold Freedom and Democracy under the God of the Earth

This book is a compilation of the lectures, with additions, as listed on
page 186.

PREFACE

This book is the Words of God who created you.

These are the Words of God—the God of ancient Africa, the Middle East and India, and the God who appears in the Old Testament and New Testament, and in the Koran. These are also the Words of the God who was revered as Supreme God Shangdi in the 5,000 years of Chinese history, the God who existed since pre-*Kojiki* times in Japanese Shinto, and the God known as Odin, the father of Mighty Thor and Loki in Northern Europe. This God is also the God of the North and South Americas.

The one and only Supreme God who stands above various ethnic gods and diverse gods—He is the highest God of the Earth who was once called "Alpha," once known as "Elohim," and is now known as "El Cantare."

Japanese people, you must change your attitude. People all over the world, accept the appearance of the Last and Greatest Savior as the Gospel.

Ryuho Okawa
Founder and CEO of Happy Science Group
December 2017

Chapter ONE

The Power to Believe

*Creating a New Reality
for Your Life and the World*

Lecture given on February 11, 2017
at Beppu International Convention Center, B-Con Plaza, Oita, Japan

1

My Lifelong Dedicated Search for the Truth

✧　✧　✧

Standing as a religious leader: I suffered from A lack of understanding by those around me

This chapter is based on the lecture I gave in Oita Prefecture, located in southern Japan, on February 11, Japan's National Foundation Day. According to various spiritual revelations given to Happy Science, the area around Oita, Kumamoto, and Miyazaki Prefectures was the main location in the founding of Japan. With that in mind, and with appreciation for Japan's continuous 2,600 or 2,700 years of history, I hope to give a glimpse of Truth in this chapter.

I gave this lecture the title, "The Power to Believe," but I do not intend to make it too difficult. By "not difficult," I do not mean the level of content will be shallow or low. Rather, I aim to make it easy to understand for a broad range of people.

More than 30 years have passed since Happy Science started its activities in 1986. I actually started receiving spiritual revelations from the heavenly world in 1981, so I have been active in this world of the Truth for 30-plus years. It undoubtedly takes some period of time. Actually, as we carried out our activities for a long time, more and more people have started to accept and understand us as something familiar.

However, during the early years of our foundation, Happy Science activities were my own matters, or matters confined only to my family or relating to the people close to me. In those days, I had all sorts of worries just like the average person. I remember struggling hard to get people to understand things that cannot be easily explained.

Usually, people will understand if someone leaves a company to work for a different company or to start another career. In my case, however, I wanted to leave my company to start a new religion, as I had been receiving revelations from the heavenly world for five or six years before then. Ten out of ten people I confided in just flatly opposed my idea.

They even asked me to show them something that could help them understand exactly what it was that I was going to do. I brought them several spiritual message books already published at that time. They included spiritual messages from the Japanese Buddhist monks Nichiren* and Kukai, Jesus Christ, and the Sun Goddess Amaterasu-O-Mikami [these are currently compiled in *Ryuho Okawa Collection of Spiritual Messages* (Tokyo: Happy Science)].

However, that only made their reaction worse. Whomever I showed the books to were at a complete loss for words, and not a

---

*Nichiren [1222-1282] was a Japanese Buddhist monk who taught devotion to the Lotus Sutra. He founded Nichiren Buddhism in 1253.

single person could give me a proper comment. Most reactions I got were, "You're lying, right? Please tell me you're lying" and "I won't tell anyone, so just tell me it's a fabrication." I could only tell them, "No, it's all true."

It was probably very difficult for them to believe that they had been working with someone who was able to hear the voices of the Sun Goddess Amaterasu-O-Mikami, Nichiren, and Jesus Christ. "This has got to be a lie" and "Give me a break"—these comments clearly showed their honest feelings. Of course, they may have heard of people with this ability historically, but those were stories of the past. Even if they could accept them as historical events, they probably could not imagine that something similar could actually happen in their environment in the present day. It was apparently a massive shock to them that one of their colleagues or acquaintances who they had spoken with, worked with, eaten with, and discussed problems with was actually such a person.

In my own family as well, there were many people who were confused soon after I started Happy Science. One response was, "We wanted at least one person in this family to be successful in this world and support this house, but you decided to go into that field? This probably happened because your father liked stories about the spiritual world." My decision was very difficult for my family and relatives. So, in the early stages, I had already experienced most of the problems that my followers who joined Happy Science a few years or decades later would experience.

Furthermore, after I left my company, I received headhuntinglike calls from various groups. I did not know where they had heard that I had quit, but some of them even called my parents' house. They would eagerly say, "We are starting a new company and we really want you to come join us" or "We'll give you twice or even three times your previous salary. We'll give you however much you ask for." I remember feeling frustrated at not being able to explain to them very well, and thought, "That's not why I quit. That's not what I want."

The realization in my early 20s: I was only Taking love from others and not giving it back

The source of my anxiety in those days was, in fact, a question as to how much I myself could believe in the voices from the heavenly world. You can find many people who are capable of hearing the voices of spirits, everywhere in Japan—especially in Okinawa and Aomori Prefectures—and in the world. Some of them serve as modest psychics in their towns, while some of the others have actually started their own religious groups. But I had absolutely no achievements, so it was only natural that I did not have confidence as to how much I could believe these spiritual voices.

I finally stood up as a religious leader at the age of 30 but, honestly speaking, as I looked back over the 30 years of my life, there was no reason why I would have to stray far in the worldly sense or live in any delusion. Of course, I went through trials and errors, but it is true that at every age and in every period of my life I strove hard to seek the Truth. I never neglected to seek the Truth and improve myself in some way. I also strove to overcome my shortcomings and mistakes to the best of my abilities, and to better my own character, my life attitude, and how I studied and worked. I tried to be someone who other people would approve of and wanted to help those in need.

Compared to how I am now, I was much more aggressive at that time; I often used strict and harsh words. Even so, deep down, I was filled with the desire to change myself to be able to contribute more to the world and do work to benefit many people. I have always been thankful to my parents who raised me to adulthood, and I always thought I had to give something back to the people who supported me.

Furthermore, I realized that while I received a lot of support from other people in the 20-plus years before entering the spiritual path, I had only given back very little in return. I keenly felt that I had just taken from others and lived a life of "taking love" during that time. I had received various things while growing up. My body and my pride had both grown large, but in terms of returning favors, I had done almost nothing. I realized this when I was in my early 20s.

I had never committed any criminal act in the worldly sense, nor do I remember purposely trying to hurt anyone. However, when I looked back over my own life up to that point, I felt, "If I were to die now, I would have only received love from other people in my life and not returned a single thing. My life was full of taking. If I were to write the love I had taken and the love I had given in my life on 'the balance sheet of love,' my life would be deep in the red. This is not good at all." Thinking about such things may sound strange to young people, but at the time, I remember looking back over my life and thinking that I had only received from other people without giving anything in return.

2

How Happy Science Developed Great Power

✧   ✧   ✧

Starting Happy Science with nothing
And struggling to run the organization

I struggled with various spiritual matters for several years as I accumulated real-world experience and, as is a common situation, was out on my own at the age of 30. At that time, there was nothing particular I could rely on—no pre-established religious group, no money, no land, no building. I had virtually nothing. The only thing I had was the support of some people who had gathered from all over Japan after reading and believing in the several books that I had so far published. Perhaps you could say they did not yet have faith at the time; they probably came out of curiosity to see the man who was working to cause spiritual and mystical phenomena.

On November 23, 1986, I gave my first lecture and started turning the Dharma Wheel. At Happy Science, we call it the Commemoration Day of the First Turning of the Dharma Wheel. Just under 90 people had gathered to listen to my lecture in Tokyo at Nippori Shuhan Kaikan [currently called Happy Science Commemoration Hall of the First Turning of the Dharma Wheel]. It was still a small audience at the time, but some of them are still active members even now. I am truly happy about that.

The room was rather small and it was packed with attendees who had come from all over the country, leaving no aisle room for me to walk through to get to the podium in the front. I remember having to go out on the narrow veranda at the side of the room to get to the front; it was as risky as walking a tightrope. I spoke most of the time during the session, which lasted almost 2 hours 40 minutes. The audience probably did not understand what was going on, and probably went home only with the premonition that something significant was going to happen. These people—a little less than 90—who showed up at this first session then became our core members.

After that, I successively held lectures and seminars, among them being the first public lecture commemorating the Foundation of Happy Science, "The Principles of Happiness," in March 8, 1987 [the lecture is now included in the book, *The Science of Happiness* (Vermont: Destiny Books, 2009)]. The first seminar, held at a venue by Lake Biwa in Shiga Prefecture in 1987 [1987 May Seminar], was attended by 108 people. Most of these 100-plus people who gathered for the seminar went on to become Happy Science staff members afterward. This shows how passionate people were in our early days. People with different career backgrounds joined us as staff members, and most of those who served as group leaders during the mealtimes at the seminar went on to become executives of Happy Science. We started out like this.

In those days, however, our staff members were not adequately trained. For this reason, in our early stages there were frequent changes in personnel as new staff members joined. We struggled over how to manage the organization, experiencing various blunders and mistakes, until things finally started to run smoothly on a larger scale. After about three years, we reached a point where we could hold lectures at fairly large venues. Thus, while the power coming down to me was quite immense and powerful, we needed to proceed slowly in our work in this world, accumulating experience and concrete achievements, so that we gained public trust.

There is a saying in the Bible, "So the last shall be first, and the first last... [Matthew 20:16, KJV]" and I experienced this numerous times. Not everyone who came to Happy Science in the early days necessarily went on to be leaders. Rather, we saw more and more people who were highly capable among those who came later, whether three years, five years, or even ten years later. The larger Happy Science grew, the more people with greater ability and talent joined. This gave birth to problems of power in the hierarchy between those who came first and those who came later. It was an opportunity for me to learn a lot about running an organization. People that I myself had never expected joined us one after the other, so there were many situations where I struggled to run the organization.

When it comes to religious belief, many people actually stumble due to some operational flaw in the group. This is true not only of Happy Science, but also of other religious groups; they stumble more in the manner of their organizational operations rather than in doubt over their teachings or doctrines. It is extremely difficult to form the foundations of an organization.

Why do Happy Science teachings Cover so many different fields?

The Happy Science group is advancing into various new fields, including politics, education, and the arts, and each time we launch into a new field, our organization goes through a period of innovation. Each time these changes occur, the nature of our organization seems to change. Then, some members who had become used to our previous way of studying and carrying out our activities suddenly get confused and lost as to what they should do.

For instance, I publish books on a variety of topics [more than 2,300 books as of November 2017], some of which are completely different in content from one another. I am certainly not trying to confuse people who support and follow us. As people in this world have a variety of careers and areas of interest, I am introducing a wide range of topics to people with different interests and different walks of life, so they can join us from any path they may be interested in. Therefore, each and every book of mine is important. Nevertheless, while some people know that, others do not.

As I mentioned in the previous section, in the early days of Happy Science, I published a spiritual message from the Sun Goddess Amaterasu-O-Mikami [now included in *Ryuho Okawa Collection of Spiritual Messages, Vols. 7 and 8* (Tokyo: Happy Science)]. A person who had helped us when we opened our first office looked at the title and asked me, "What is *Tenteru Daijin*[*]?" This was a great shock to me. Apparently, she had never even heard of Amaterasu-O-Mikami. While it is true that the Japanese postwar education system no longer teaches children about historical myths and beliefs, I never imagined someone would misread the name Amaterasu-O-Mikami as Tenteru Daijin. I could not help but be speechless.

Japan has almost completely omitted its myths and religious beliefs from education. What is more, over half of the schools officially permitted to operate as religious schools are Christian. This is why the number of people who do not know much about Japanese traditional beliefs is growing. I launched Happy Science and conducted activities for over 30 years amid such an environment.

[*] The Chinese characters for Amaterasu-O-Mikami can be mistakenly read as Tenteru Daijin.

Great miracles like none in the past
Will occur from now on

I have now accumulated much experience. From the first room we rented that was 10 sq. meters [about 108 sq. ft.], we have now grown into an organization that has over 700 buildings. If we total our local branches, missionary centers, and missionary houses including rented space, we have about 10,000 facilities all over the world. Each location has a potential to grow larger with further investment in human resources and funding. All we have to do now is to keep pushing forward with these activities. I believe what we have achieved so far has only been the first half of our activities. From now on, in the second half, great miracles like none in the past will occur much more clearly.

I am the type of person who goes about things in an extremely logical manner, so I wait until the basic framework is set before making something larger. But once I have created a certain framework, I move fast. So, from now on, in the second half, Happy Science will definitely gain even more power in a way we have never seen before. Even those at the epicenter, or the leaders in our organization, will be surprised by the change. The "amateur age" we have been in until now has ended and a new "professional age" will begin from now. You can be sure about this.

Happy Science is creating major trends in Japan

While we still have a long way to go, Happy Science has now become the most competitive religious group in Japan before we knew it. Maybe "competitive" is not the right word, but we have become an advanced religion with foresight in a variety of fields, compared to traditional religions which have become obsolete and archaic as well as new religious groups that have appeared in these past several decades. Just looking at the activities of Happy Science, some may doubt if we are truly a religion, or argue that our political movement is not too successful. Some people may view us this way, but many of our suggestions are actually being adopted and implemented successively after being taken up by various politicians, political groups and parties. What we have been saying is eventually becoming true.

Now, Happy Science is a major pillar of theoretical ideas in Japan. To tell the truth, even people who do not belong to the Happiness Realization Party [HRP] [see end section p.198 for more information] study the various concepts of Happy Science. Many people including politicians, government officials and those in mass media study my books, so we are actually creating an invisible subculture in Japan. It may not be obvious from the outside, but right now Happy Science is creating major trends in Japan. So, by reading books published by Happy Science, you are able to see what is going on in the world and how events will unfold.

For example, in February 2017, Japanese Prime Minister Abe visited the White House to meet U.S. President Trump, and went to

Florida to play golf with him. It is quite taxing to get on a non-stop flight to Washington D.C., have lunch, fly to Florida on Airforce One, play golf, and fly back to Japan right away without much rest. His physical stamina deserves respect; an average company employee could hardly do the same. Prime Minister Abe is giving it his all because his work will end if or when he gives up.

He is doing this probably because, since the beginning of 2016, I frequently put out the message, "In the U.S., the Trump administration will come next. It will be 'The Trump Revolution,' so Japan must follow this trend. Japan must let go of any attachments and steer in that direction." As a result, Japan is moving in the direction I indicated. I believe this, itself, is a good thing. We can accept others achieving good results, even if those are based on our ideas.

Influencing the world
With our way of thinking, ideals, and power of thought

While it is OK for other political parties to implement HRP policies, I hope people will support the HRP more, so that we will be able to get some seats in the Japanese National Assembly. For example, Russian President Putin's true feeling is that he wants to resolve the Northern Territories problem and sign a treaty with Japan, but he cannot trust the current government. He most probably thinks that he can only trust Happy Science and the HRP. He studies our books such as spiritual interviews with guardian spirits, so he knows our thoughts and policies [see *A New Message from Vladimir Putin: Interviewing the Guardian Spirit of the President of Russia* (New York: IRH Press, 2014), *Putin's Insights on Russia, Japan and the World: An Interview with the Guardian Spirit of the President of Russia* (Tokyo: HS Press, 2016), and *Russia no Honne: Putin Daitoryo Shugorei vs. Okawa Yuta* (literally, "Russia's True Thoughts: The Guardian Spirit of President Putin vs. Yuta Okawa") (Tokyo: IRH Press, 2016)].

In one of those books, his guardian spirit takes a provocative stance stating, "I want to solve the territorial issues with Japan but I cannot do that as long as the current Japanese politics remains the same. If the Japanese government forms a coalition with the HRP, I would not mind returning the northern islands." I want to try something. Please keep this in mind.

After all, Russia also has an intelligence network. About two or three years ago, when several students of Happy Science Academy Nasu Main Campus submitted their works in an art exhibition held in Khabarovsk, Russia [an international festival of children and youth artistic creativity, "The Russian Far East and Asia Pacific Region: The Great Pacific Ocean of Friendship and Dream"], they won prizes and their pieces were exhibited in Russia. Based solely on this connection, students from a Russian school visited Happy Science Academy Nasu Main Campus in goodwill and friendship, and took part in cultural exchanges. Setting up this kind of relationship is quite rare, so someone from the Russian government was probably involved. Thus, interaction with Russia has been progressing under the surface.

In the U.S., even before the beginning of the Trump administration, when people were saying his chances were overwhelmingly negative, our staff members in Happy Science International Headquarters and the HRP had conversations with his advisor, who later attended my lecture in New York on October 2, 2016 [see Figure 1]. I was given the same cuff links that President Trump wears, through this advisor.

As these examples show, Happy Science now has significant influence in the U.S., Russia, and other areas under the surface. We are actually driving real world politics forward. This means that what we are doing is neither wrong nor irrelevant, but is beginning to affect the world through our way of thinking, ideals, and power of thought. It may take a little more time until we start influencing things in a way people can actually see, but that will gradually take shape.

Figure 1.
A photo of the main venue of the lecture, "Freedom, Justice, and Happiness" given on October 2, 2016 in New York [Crowne Plaza Times Square Manhattan].

3

Carrying Out Activities
To End Wars Around the World

✧   ✧   ✧

Being at an important turning point of the era

February 11 is National Foundation Day in Japan, while in South Africa, Nelson Mandela was released on that date in 1990 after serving 27 years in prison. Happy Science published a spiritual interview with Mandela, who many people may know of, under the title, *Nelson Mandela's Last Message to the World* [New York: IRH Press, 2013]. We also launched the "HS Nelson Mandela Fund"*to carry out various international activities, and many people are supporting this fund.

Mandela was released about the same time I began to give large public lectures at venues like Makuhari Messe in Chiba Prefecture. He then went on to become the president and succeeded in the grand endeavor to unite a nation that was divided into black and white South Africans. A man who was deemed a kind of terrorist by the former white government for having engaged in the movement

---

*The HS Nelson Mandela Fund, an internal fund of the Happy Science Group, was established in 2013 to provide support for the people who are unable to receive proper education and medication as a result of racial discrimination and the caste system.

to free black people completed a 27-year prison term, and after his release became the president and united a divided nation.

Right now, many mass media outlets warn that the U.S. might become divided because of President Trump, but I do not believe this will actually occur; quite the opposite will probably happen. I expect the U.S. to return to its previous status and protect the world as "a teacher of the world." The role Japan will have to play at that time will likely become far bigger than what it has been so far. Japan will be an essential partner to the U.S.

In everything, way of thinking comes first. How should we think? Gods and highly divine spirits in the heavenly world are sending down various teachings to this current age. In addition, I want people to understand why so many teachings are being delivered to Japan from the heavenly world now. Historically, this is a rare occurrence; it means we are currently at an important turning point of the era.

Working to eradicate the root cause of religious wars

Happy Science has received messages from over 700 spiritual beings to date. We have published more than 450 books on spiritual messages alone [as of November 2017], many of which have been translated and published in foreign languages and read in many countries. They have especially penetrated quite deeply into countries with strong religious faith. In Japan, more people are skeptical about spiritual messages, but people in countries that believe in spiritual matters seem to accept our spiritual messages from the heart, quite easily and straightforwardly.

My teachings include the following. "The world is divided into various religions, such as Buddhism, Christianity, Confucianism, Taoism, Islam, Hinduism, and Japanese Shinto. They originated independently in times when the means of transportation and communication were still limited. They were founded for their own people native to certain geographic areas, but nowadays, we need teachings that can integrate all the advanced religions in the world. Under such teachings, we must once again bring people of different races who believe in various religions together on equal footing that will allow them to understand each other, so that they can have discussions."

I also speak on national defense, of course, because it is important in the practical sense. As a religion, we are saying conflict and slaughter that arise from differences in religion are utterly futile. By disclosing the original intent, the true meaning behind the foundations of Christianity and Islam, I am trying to eradicate the root cause of conflicts.

Providing logical philosophies
To overcome potential wars in Asia

China became an atheist country and proclaimed that religion was the opium, ever since Marxism was introduced there. Mao Zedong, for example, invaded Tibet and began the oppression of Buddhism there. Nonetheless, traditional Chinese thought acknowledges the existence of Shangdi, or the emperor in Heaven. The idea of an emperor in Heaven, in other words, one that acknowledges the existence of God, has continued unbroken for several thousands of years in China, so it is not true to say that Chinese people do not believe in God. In general, most Chinese people do have various religious beliefs, including Shenxian thought [the belief in the existence of immortal sennins or hermits], Taoist thought, Buddhist thought, and recently, Christianity and partially Happy Science. Currently, an outstanding Light has descended to Taiwan as well.*

There are also problems on the Korean Peninsula, which involves North and South Korea. I definitely want to help resolve the existing Korean conflict while I am still on earth. We do not know exactly how people in North Korea view the situation or how they have been taught and brainwashed by their government, but they

---

*Just after the presidential election in Taiwan in 2016, Okawa conducted a spiritual interview with the guardian spirit of its new President Tsai Ing-wen. In the interview, her guardian spirit revealed that she has a great mission ahead of her. Published as *Kinkyu Shugorei Interview: Taiwan Shin Soto Tsai Ing-wen no Mirai Senryaku* [literally, "Urgent Guardian Spirit Interview: New Taiwanese President Tsai Ing-wen's Future Strategy" (Tokyo: IRH Press, 2016)].

are undoubtedly unhappy in their present situation. People in South Korea also seem to find it difficult to make clear their own direction. While holding a fiery sense of opposition toward the North, they sometimes are pro-Chinese and anti-Japanese or anti-U.S., but then at times reverse their attitudes. I truly want these major issues of North and South Korea and of China to be resolved during my time.

For the time being, however, difficult days will continue. China has built a three-kilometer-long [about two miles] airstrip in the South China Sea by pouring concrete onto a reef, making it possible to launch aerial bombing operations from there. With the rise of President Trump in the U.S., I presume that a regional war could well break out within four or five years. I do not think we will see the Spratly Islands issue developing into a military conflict as massive as what the North Korean or Taiwanese issues may develop into, but there is a strong chance that we will eventually see local conflicts or wars breaking out.

For this reason, Japan should also realize the importance of national defense. At the same time, it must have philosophies logical enough to overcome those issues. The current Abe administration holds that Japan should build up its national defense to a more practical level, and I agree to some extent. Happy Science has definitely played a major role in providing the government with logic regarding Japan's national defense.

Mere arguments over World War II, which occurred 70 or 80 years ago, will never help Japan move forward with its defense issues; such arguments will only help politicians make convenient excuses for themselves. I believe we need philosophies that allow people to overcome past problems and move forward, and Happy Science provides just those. We want this unstable region of Asia to become stable in the future.

Forgiveness and reconciliation are possible Only because there is the Being greater than humans

It is true that Marxist thinking includes ideas that are sympathetic toward the weak. However, the materialistic thought in it that claims, "Only physical and material things exist in this world" is clearly wrong. As someone who experienced receiving different kinds of spiritual guidance and messages over the past 30 years or so, I can say that materialism is undoubtedly wrong. Materialism is an idea that I can never approve of, and I am fundamentally opposed to the idea that religion is opium or poison.

In essence, human character and morality will not improve without God. Humans are able to have lofty feelings by believing in something greater than themselves, something greater than humans. Those who hate each other can forgive and reconcile only because there is the Being superior to them.

Happy Science philosophies also incorporate such principles of forgiveness. We do not want to create conflict or instigate war. Sometimes we give advice to political leaders to prepare against potential dangers, but we do so not because we want to wage war.

We do so to prevent those with evil intentions from attempting evil deeds. My primary message is that if seeds of conflict lie in people's different ideas, then we must overcome them with thoughts of a larger scale. I have been repeatedly stating the importance of this.

4

The Power to Believe Will Work Miracles

✧   ✧   ✧

Happy Science is spreading into Asia and Africa as well

People in countries with strong faith sometimes understand the value of Happy Science teachings far more deeply than Japanese people. In 2011, for example, I gave a lecture in India. I held an outdoor lecture in Bodh Gaya, addressing an audience of more than 40,000 people [see Figure 2].

The Mahabodhi Temple is a large temple located beside a massive Bodhi tree that is apparently the third or fourth-generation offspring plant of the one under which Shakyamuni Buddha attained enlightenment over 2,500 years ago. Monks from the Mahabodhi Temple were seated near the center of the first and second rows of the audience, so I gave the lecture with them in mind.

The lecture venue was set up under a vast tent-like structure, which enabled us to fit about 40,000 people inside. But even after the lecture started, more and more people kept trying to push their way in to somehow get inside. I remember there were continuous lines of people who had walked barefoot from miles around to come hear me speak.

When I gave a lecture in Uganda in 2012 [see Figure 3], there were also a very large number of people gathered at an international stadium to hear my lecture. Apparently, there was a squall [a sudden localized storm] during the pre-lecture program and some of the audience left the stadium to take shelter in buses. But when we were going to start the lecture, we could not call them back because we

Figure 2.
A photo of the lecture, "The Real Buddha and New Hope" given on March 6, 2011 in Bodh Gaya, India, where over 40,000 people gathered at the Kalachakra square.

had no PA system in the stadium to make an announcement. As a result, the people taking shelter from the squall were unable to attend my lecture. Another problem we had was that more than 100 buses from different areas did not show up as scheduled.

In addition, the people in the stadium listened to my lecture with plastic chairs on their heads to cover themselves from the rain. It was a little hard to find a good scene to show, but I heard that the national broadcasting stations there broadcast my lecture quite nicely. Later, the people who missed my lecture became very upset, so it was rebroadcast several times throughout Uganda and its neighboring countries on different television channels. The number of people who listened to my lecture in Africa reportedly amounted to somewhere between 30 to 50 million, including those who viewed

Figure 3.
A photo of the lecture, "The Light of New Hope" given on June 23, 2012 in Uganda, Africa [Mandela National Stadium in Kampala].

it on television broadcasts outside Uganda. Thus, my name is now highly recognized in Africa.

In other Asian countries as well, such as Hong Kong, wherever I went, people would come up to ask me to take pictures with them.[*] It has happened numerous times overseas, but not in Japan, though it might partly be due to differences in national character. The examples above show that Happy Science is actually becoming well-known around the world.

The difficulty of being accepted by society

The Japanese mass media are nevertheless very biased in their coverage. President Trump has made enemies of the American mass media by saying that they are reporting fake news. While his comments seem provocative, I have been pointing out this problem with the media quite often, too, and I find his ideas to be similar to mine. He is voicing his opinions in an extremely frank and honest fashion, but the mass media probably interpret and report his words only in a negative way.

The instinct of the mass media is to oppose those in power and, as an unwritten rule, they have a mission to stand up against any person who has the potential to wield despotic power. It is good

---

[*] The author has also given lectures in other parts of Asia, such as South Korea, Taiwan, Nepal, the Philippines, Hong Kong, Singapore, Malaysia, and Sri Lanka.

that they sometimes attempt to challenge these people and see what happens. However, President Trump has continuously been accused from day one, despite the media's general rule of refraining from criticism during the first hundred days of a new president's term, called the "honeymoon period." President Trump has been working hard amidst constant criticism.

Looking at the situation, it is apparent that even in the U.S., it is very difficult to gain everyone's understanding. Even though Donald Trump became president after having won the election, which was according to democratic rules, some people continue to display acts of resistance and rally to denounce him. This makes me feel that the U.S., too, has become more like a non-democratic nation. It is truly difficult to be accepted by society.

Great outside power will come To those who have faith as they make efforts

While many people are now silently watching and supporting Happy Science, some may still be afraid to accept our opinions straightforwardly or wholeheartedly. However, here I want to emphasize that we are basically filled with the desire to save as many people as possible. We want to help people.

My wish is that people develop or rebuild themselves on their own as long as they can, and for people who have managed to make themselves stronger and wealthier to stretch out a helping hand to those who are unable to do so. Some people may think that big government should step in to do everything to help people, but unfortunately, in many cases, various countries in the world show us that this does not actually work. So, it is important that people do what they can on their own.

However, while I want people to make efforts to help themselves, I also want them to remember the outside power. By believing, great power will come from the heavenly world to save people. At Happy Science, many miracles actually occur on various occasions. Among those who believe, some have experienced miracles. Hundreds or even thousands of illnesses have already been cured, too. They continue to be cured even today. This is indeed a mysterious phenomenon.

We do not advertise these kinds of miracles much because we think it is a natural consequence. We are not attempting to cure illnesses in place of doctors; rather, the person's faith is actually healing his or her illness. With the consent of heavenly beings, when the person's faith receives a response from the heavenly world, his or her illness is miraculously cured. Miracles only occur under this circumstance.

Apart from illnesses, many Happy Science members have also recovered from economic problems. In these last 30 years or so, many have succeeded in growing their companies into major corporations. Those who have read my books, including non-members, have achieved success by launching their own businesses.

We are seeing positive results in education as well. When a school principal was appointed to a new school, he happened to find my book, *Kyoiku no Ho* [literally, "The Laws of Education" (Tokyo: IRH Press, 2011)], already shelved in the principal's office. I hear that the book is being studied in many schools in Japan. A large number of people in the field of education are studying the new educational ideals proposed by Happy Science.

The Happiness Realization Party is openly active, Without hiding its connection to Happy Science

While Happy Science members are active in a visible way, there are also great numbers of non-members who understand and support our ideas. I hope these people will eventually confidently declare that they want to help, support and join our activities. We need to create an organization that is overflowing with confidence and courage and that would allow them to make that statement. This is what we must do now. I hope people from different backgrounds can declare their faith willingly and openly say, "I am a Happy Science believer. I have confidence in my faith."

The Happiness Realization Party chooses to carry out its activities without hiding its connection to Happy Science. We need strong and confident people who can win elections without hiding the name "Happy Science," rather than weak ones who hesitate to mention the name in fear of losing. The first attempt to run as an HRP candidate may certainly be frightening, but continued attempts will reveal their true characters, and people will definitely start to understand the candidates' policies and objectives.

A master of self-realization once said that those who give up after one failure are mediocre, those who do not give up after three failures are outstanding, and those who do not give up after ten failures are geniuses. This being so, the HRP candidates are quite close to genius level. They will most likely be among the geniuses. I believe the more one loses in elections, the more his or her true ability will manifest.

There are actually HRP supporters in different arenas, but many still support other parties, believing that it is safer to leave real politics to long-standing political names. The current small electoral district system tends to converge into the two-party system, leaving little chance for other small parties to win. Even so, I believe HRP will gradually find a way to gain public favor. In the end, my hope is for the entire population of Japan to become our followers, so we just have to keep striving toward that goal. I believe everything is moving forward.

The power to believe: its true meaning

Not many people may yet understand the true meaning of the power to believe. The power to believe is not something that only serves to ease our heart; it truly has a physical power to break through and penetrate any obstacle that is blocking the paths of each person's life in this world.

Among the so-called intellectuals today, many advocate agnosticism and state, "We cannot know the truth about this world. We cannot know about God. We cannot know about the beginning of this world. We cannot know about spirits or the Spirit World." But the power of belief will make a breakthrough, as if boring a tunnel through the mountains of those agnostic crowds who cannot believe in any spiritual matters. We can cut through any barrier by concentrating this power of belief like a laser beam.

I believe now is the time to do this. To those who believe in Happy Science around the world, all who support or take interest in Happy Science, and all who will join us in the future—if you can believe there is some truth in what I have been doing these past 30-plus years, please turn your power of thought into a strong light that can bore a tunnel through the mountains blocking our future and the power of God. I want to create such a massive trend. I await the day when all of your power comes together as one.

The Limitless Power of Faith, And the Miracles to Cure Illnesses

Your environment,
Personality and future will change
If you transform your mind.
The fundamental power behind this
Is the power of faith.

Faith is very much like connecting your home
To the main water supply;
Turning on the tap will allow the water to flow
From the main supply to your house.
That is faith.
Even if there is abundant water in the main supply,
Unless you "turn on the tap" with your faith,
Water will not flow.
Similarly, through believing,
Affirming and accepting,
You shall be given limitless power.

The power of belief is
Something that is not usually taught in schools.
You can only learn it
Through religion or religious education.

Just as your true Father
Is limitless and invincible in Heaven,
So must you be,
Limitless and invincible here on earth.
This is what it means to win in terms of faith.

People's illnesses can be cured through faith.
The fundamental structure of your physical body
Will change depending on your life's views
And your self-image.

Your red and white blood cells
As well as the lymphocytes in your blood
Are also active every day
While receiving a powerful spiritual life force.
Their activities will change

With the kind of thoughts you emit.

They will start to fight viruses
And other harmful things within you,
Expelling them from your body.
Cancerous cells and other inappropriate tissues
Will be rapidly replaced and disposed of
Through your thoughts.
They will be weeded out.

Chapter TWO

Starting from Love

*Solve Life's Problems and Become
An Expert in the Study of Life*

Lecture given on July 9, 2017
at Tokyo Shoshinkan, Tokyo, Japan

1

The Desire to be Loved
Is a Human Instinct

✧　　✧　　✧

Humans naturally want to be loved

The theme of this chapter, "Starting from Love," is a concept that I often used to teach in the early days of Happy Science, so those who have been with us since the beginning may feel nostalgic, as if we have gone back in time. That was when I was a lot younger. Although I am still young at heart, actually decades have passed since I spoke frequently on the topic. So, you may wonder if and how my teachings on love have changed since then.

When thinking about love, young people in general tend to think that love determines whether they are happy or unhappy. They are happy when they are loved by others and unhappy when they are not. This is the initial and most basic feeling. People tend to feel this way instinctively without being taught; some may start feeling this way from the early to late teen years.

Young people, in particular, have a strong desire to be loved by others and, if they go further, want to keep that love only for themselves. They want someone to love only them. This is often the theme of many TV dramas.

If this desire for love works positively, it can inspire you to achieve self-realization. You would want to develop yourself more, become a better person and be respected by others. You would seek praise from the one you admire and want to have all of his or her attention to yourself. This is not necessarily a bad thing. Many people in their middle age or their prime might still have such feelings, too.

The desire for love can be a driving force to try hard

With the population growing, competition for love has become very intense. Popular people attract the admiration of many people, but although they could love a lot of people in a shallow and wide manner, building deep, meaningful love with one person is another matter. On the other hand, if a person seeks love from another person who does not get much attention, the other person may be quick to respond. In general, popular people are always popular while those who are not popular stay that way.

This may not be an appropriate example to cite, but sadly enough, candidates of the Happiness Realization Party get fewer votes in elections compared to those of other parties. It causes me to wonder why, and makes me want to call for some love [*laughs*]. It truly puzzles me why we only get so few votes. Indeed, it would be nice to get as much "love" and "equal results" as other parties do.

Even though we believe we are giving out love, we do not feel that love is being returned. This is our general feeling in our daily lives. Young people, in particular, cannot measure their own worth or see their brilliance objectively, so they often suffer from a gap between the way they want things to be and reality. As a result, they naturally develop a strong desire to stand out from everyone else. But this also serves as a driving force for them to do their best in sports, work or study, so it is not necessarily a bad thing.

Even if you do not have the looks or academic abilities, you could, for example, be an ace pitcher in baseball. If you get a chance to pitch at a high school baseball tournament and your game is broadcast nationally, you may become the center of attention and be popular among the girls at your school.

Perhaps you could succeed in making a name for yourself in the entertainment world. Happy Science is also involved in entertainment production. Some people may wish to be like the actors whose faces appear on the big screen. However, they will realize it is extremely hard to achieve such levels of success in reality.

The desire to be loved can be a source of suffering

The effort you put into self-improvement during your youth is usually largely based on your yearning to get attention from others, or more simply, to be loved by others. I am not trying to deny this desire altogether. But while it is true that this can be used as a springboard for advancement, unfortunately, it often brings suffering.

Looking at the world around us, you will rarely meet people who come to you and offer you love. Rather, when someone approaches you, you quickly assume that he or she wants something from you. Happy Science members also do missionary work and election campaigning, so I feel we must open up a little more to such people. Nevertheless, oftentimes when people approach you on the street, they usually want something from you.

In public, there are people who distribute flyers along with free pocket tissues,* but even so, not many passersby take them. The value of a pack of pocket tissues is not zero, so taking it is not completely useless. But just thinking about how the tissues would stuff your pocket sometimes makes you uninterested in accepting them.

People do not even take free pocket tissues, so I am sure our members are also struggling in their missionary work on the street. Our members might stand in front of a station and ask passersby, "Are you interested in Happy Science?" or "Don't you have worries?" but the passersby may well avoid our members or say, "Leave me alone."

Most people might feel it would be nice to be on TV, but when they actually see a few camera and TV crew huddling near an intersection, they will most likely avoid the camera. I would do the same. If I were to be on a TV show, it would be free publicity and a free ad for Happy Science, but just imagine people seeing Ryuho

---

* In major cities in Japan, many businesses advertise themselves by passing out their flyers along with free pocket tissues.

Okawa caught at an intersection for a casual interview on TV, for example, "Where are you going?" "Just over there. I'm hungry, so I'm going out for noodles." If such an interview was shown on nationwide TV, my followers would be disappointed. It might be better if the interview covered higher-level topics, but that usually is not the case. So, offers by TV crews are often declined by people on the street.

Various situations that make it difficult to love others

About 10 years ago, a new donut shop opened, and it was featured in magazines as a trendy new store. So, I went soon after it opened. It happened to be raining that day and there were no customers. There was a camera crew waiting there, ready to report on the new shop bustling with customers, but it was empty. When I walked in, I was leaped on like some kind of prey by a reporter who asked, "Excuse me, can we interview you please?"

When I politely refused, the interviewer was disappointed and went outside despondently. I felt sorry for him and thought that it might have done some good for the shop if I accepted the interview, but I decided not to because I did not think I was the right person to appear in their publicity. It might have caused problems for the shop if it then became flooded with Happy Science members.

I can see how people in the media industry get nastier as they are turned down many times in this way. It may make them want to say something that causes offense or anger. In TV programs as well as weekly magazines, they are often refused when seeking to interview people. As they experience their "love" being rejected many times, apparently, they often develop a negative side to their characters. I can understand that.

People in general, on the other hand, are scared when a candid shot captures them unprepared, even if they want to appear on TV or other media. It is only natural for people to want to show their good side, but not their embarrassing aspects. By the way, when I am relaxed and enjoying myself at home, my wife takes a lot of candid photos of me. Apparently, she stores them under lock and key, so no one else can see them. She enjoys them in private, but I hope they will not be made public [*laughs*].

Anyhow, there are difficult aspects in building positive relationships with others because even if you want to develop a better relationship with someone, an unexpected situation can arise to block your way. The same can be true in loving someone. Two people loving each other is not something that happens all that easily. For example, it is difficult for young people who are attracted to one another to stay together even after encountering some obstacles. This being the case for romantic love, I truly feel it is all the more difficult to love others beyond the scope of those one knows, such as strangers or the general public.

2

The Pain of Love
That Comes with Life's Problems
And Organizational Management

✧　　✧　　✧

Various problems come with parental and marital love

Since our early days at Happy Science, we have been teaching that life is a workbook of problems to be solved. Perhaps you could say that love is a very typical issue in this workbook of life; each and every one of us will inevitably face it.

For example, the love between a man and a woman starts relatively early in life. Then, when people have offspring, they face troubles that deal with the love between parents and children. Many conflicts occur; sometimes the more you love your children, the more they rebel against you later on. In this way, love can turn into something quite the opposite. On the other hand, there are cases where the children do surprisingly well and turn out to be dutiful sons or daughters despite their parents' low expectations or little affection. The parent-child relationship is indeed very difficult.

The love between husband and wife also gives rise to various problems. Even if their love was true and sincere when they were young, circumstances can change as they reach middle age or later;

their conditions at work can change or other responsibilities may come up in addition to raising their children.

Take, for example, a Happy Science believer who is a homemaker and a mother. If her family members are also believers, she may be able to attend Happy Science lecture on a Sunday without any concern, but what if her son has an important exam that will determine whether he can enter his first school of choice and desperately wants the full support from his mother to achieve the highest possible score? Under such extreme tension and anxiety that he believes might determine his future, if his mother tells him that she is going away for the lecture on the day before his exam, he might get upset and claim that his mother does not think about him at all. Then, they might get into an argument where she says, "Are you denying my faith?" to which the son replies, "No, I can understand, but my exam is also important!" As your children get older, things change and become more difficult to deal with.

A similar argument can come up with her husband. He might say, "I have an appointment with my clients to play golf today, and I cannot miss it. You may want to go to Master's lecture, but I cannot cancel my golf appointment to support our son instead. For me, my clients take priority. It is because of my salary that you are all able to eat and take part in religious activities. So, today's golf is important! Even if something happens to Master Okawa, my golf comes first!" Then she might want to retort, "You lack faith!"

I presume many Happy Science members have had this kind of conflict with their spouses, but this cannot be helped. Life is limited and you have to consider how to use the few decades of your life to make your life shine brightly. When you consider what would make your life meaningful, you have to prioritize what you feel is valuable.

Then, the mother could think, "There is little I can do today to help my son improve his exam score; the result would be the same, with or without my support" or "My son is just taking out his frustration on me." Alternatively, she could think, "My husband is free to go golfing. If he has to let the clients win, then so be it. It's up to him. It has little to do with my attending Master's lecture."

The examples above show that even in relationships that began with pure love, you may well undergo various kinds of misunderstandings or miscommunications as your life experience deepens.

The pain of not being understood regarding Personnel management for Happy Science's development

I have been managing Happy Science for more than 30 years, and the most painful experience during that time was to see my disciples, who I loved, walk away due to some kind of misunderstanding. The sorrow I felt was indeed indescribable.

For instance, people who helped us in the early days of Happy Science were very devoted; they worked hard and selflessly to carry out our mission. But as the organization grew, our scope of work became difficult to manage and we needed new people with different abilities. Even though they joined later, it was necessary to employ them to be able to manage the organization. However, when new members were placed in important positions, those who had been with us from earlier times began to feel neglected; some lost motivation or became frustrated, while others decided to quit.

It did not mean that I stopped loving them, of course. I was grateful to them for working hard and appreciated their help. My feelings never changed. Still, in order to develop our organization, I needed to find and place, at each given time, appropriate people in appropriate positions; otherwise, I would have had to give up what I felt was right. So, I had to do it, but oftentimes people did not understand my intentions.

In fact, people tend to love others only when they are appreciated. Continuously loving others regardless of whether you are appreciated or not is indeed a difficult thing to do. That is because you do not fully understand what the other person thinks. When you are told you are trusted or loved, you tend to think that everything about you should be loved or that you should be trusted in everything you do. For this reason, many people suddenly become offended when their work is corrected, rejected, or replaced. I have experienced deep sorrow regarding this numerous times in the past.

The difficulty of organizational management: Saint Francis of Assisi and Mother Teresa

In order to talk about love, I felt the need for some study of Christianity, so the day before giving the lecture on which this chapter is based, I again watched a movie about Saint Francis of Assisi from the medieval period who founded a religious order in Italy in the early 1200s, and a movie about Mother Teresa starring Olivia Hussey. In both movies, I found that while the leaders were freely doing whatever they wanted in their own ways, things became increasingly difficult as they gained more followers.

In the case of Francis of Assisi, when his members grew to a few thousand people across many countries, he was asked to set up regulations and qualifications for becoming a member, but he did not want to. Although he needed to do this and get approval from the pope, he did not want to do it.

It is certainly true that a leader needs to get more knowledgeable people involved and utilize them to manage an organization well. There were universities in 13th-century Italy, and intellectuals who had studied grammar, theology and law actually approached Francis and insisted he use them. But Francis said that although these people were indeed eloquent, they did not have faith, which was the most important thing, and stated that just following the Gospels was more than enough. The movie depicted how he had suffered because he did not set up regulations.

Similar problems were depicted in the movie about Mother Teresa starring Olivia Hussey. Incidentally, Sri Lankan actress Umali Thilakarathne who starred in our movie, *The Final Judgement* [executive producer Ryuho Okawa, released in 2012], played the role of an assistant to Mother Teresa. Mother Teresa was the kind of person who acted impulsively, and she would infringe the law and regulations on various occasions, creating conflict with the government. Such actions often became obstacles that blocked her from carrying out her work.

Watching these movies made me feel how difficult it is to build and expand an organization because the process often involves confrontations with worldly matters. Religious leaders wonder why people do not understand them when they just want to spread God's Love. People around them point out, for example, that according to regulations, they cannot build an orphanage unless they get official approval. These are the troubles they face. After re-watching these two movies, I again felt how difficult it was to manage an organization.

The difficulty of practicing "nurturing love" In organizational management: Shakyamuni Buddha

Shakyamuni Buddha also experienced the same kind of difficulty. In the beginning, when he and his disciples underwent spiritual training freely in the forest, each person was training in his own way. But as the Sangha [group of disciples] formed into an organization, many problems and conflicts arose, and it was difficult to decide who was right.

Shakyamuni Buddha made it a rule that four renunciant disciples form a small group [*sammukhībhūta-samgha*, or *Genzen-Sangha* in Japanese] to make decisions about what was right or wrong [this way of judgment is also called *karman*, or *Komma* in Japanese]. But sometimes they could not make decisions. There were matters so complex that even Shakyamuni Buddha would give up deciding what was right.

When managing an organization, it is a battle of human egos, and there will be some disagreement in what each member thinks is right or good. In addition, when adjustments begin to work, things may not necessarily abide by the simple principle of love. Love seemingly accepts all, forgives all, and embraces all, but as we live in the realities of this world, there are times when we must make many adjustments and decisions, as well as choose one thing and give up another. This is a very difficult aspect which is part of the practice called "nurturing love" in the theory of the developmental stages of love.* When you have gained knowledge and wisdom, you must set priorities to these difficult problems from the perspective of Buddha's Truth, but at this stage, you may often face difficulties regarding a primitive stage of love.

---

*Happy Science teaches that there are different levels of love, ranging from "fundamental love" to "love of saviors." Refer to *The Laws of the Sun* [New York: IRH Press, 2013] for more details on the developmental stages of love.

Happy Science has grown very large in the 31 years since its founding, and is now spreading internationally. Among those who helped us during the initial stages, there are some who are still helping us even now, without having their pride get in the way. These people must be truly happy and honored to see Happy Science grow to be what it is now. I feel the same way.

On the other hand, there were also some, in the initial stages of Happy Science, who were offended or mistakenly thought that they were no longer loved when newer members replaced them. Some even returned the gifts we had given without opening them. I felt they were very simple-minded people who took things on an all-or-nothing basis. This is a difficult attitude to have in a work setting, but it actually happened.

3

Become a Professional in the Study of Life By Learning to Love and Believe

✧　　✧　　✧

Overcome each koan *that appears in your life,*
One at a time

With regard to the love between a man and a woman, too, many kinds of drama can occur in a decades-long marital life. Even if a couple is doing well, their opinions may differ over relations with their children or others, or an unlawful incident may one day occur within the family.

In 2017, a Japanese TV drama featured a man who had been concealing his incompetency at work from his pregnant wife, who believed him to be a capable worker. This could happen in real life. When a woman marries in her 20s, she may speak proudly how handsome and capable her husband is among the elite. But in her 30s, she may come to realize that in fact he is actually useless at work. This is scary but true.

There are cases where husband and wife are both working, and the wife quickly advances in her career and gains higher recognition. Then the husband gets frustrated and acts like a rebellious child. This is also a difficult issue. Once finding her vocation, it is only natural that the woman wants to be recognized and wants to contribute to society as a working adult. But if she is successful, her husband will gradually behave like an unruly juvenile. If she does not have a career, she can live in harmony with her husband, but if she ambitiously advances in her career, they cannot stay together as a married couple. This is painful.

Such *koan*-like* difficult issues, which require deep contemplation, arise on various occasions in life. We need to overcome them, one by one.

One of the significances of studying religious teachings Is to become a professional in the study of life

A lot of life's problems can be solved, but not all of them. When solving problems, your choice of one option may mean giving up another. It is truly painful. However, various difficulties are bound to occur to some extent as part of the workbook of problems on love. In truth, God created men and women to have them learn about love. Everyone is destined to encounter such problems.

Nevertheless, as you attempt to work out many of those problems, you may find that your love, which was initially pure and innocent, changes into something slightly different. For example, our next movie, *Daybreak* [executive producer Ryuho Okawa, to

---

* *Koan* is a contemplative question originated in Zen Buddhism, but also common in Happy Science. The practitioners strive to solve it through deep contemplation.

be released early summer in 2018 in Japan] has the theme song, "Through the Sleepless Nights" [lyrics and music by Ryuho Okawa]. It is a song about the main characters' emotional struggles caused by not being able to marry. There are times when you suffer because you cannot be with the one you love. Yet, once you get married, you will be met with new kinds of struggle. We must confront such problems, one at a time, otherwise we will not be able to solve them.

Even so, at some point, you may find that you cannot solve them all. At that time, please consider the significance of studying religious teachings in life. Your study of religious teachings means that you have made up your mind to become a professional in the study of human life for the sake of providing answers to other people's problems in life. This may well be one of the reasons that you encountered Happy Science. How you overcome or persevere through your own personal problems is crucial if you wish to be someone who can guide others in solving their life's problems.

Keep believing even when miracles do not happen

There are times when a miracle may happen to you; you may actually recover from an illness. There are such "chosen people," but even they may later become ill again and pass away. For example, an illness cured by a miracle 10 years earlier may not be cured the second time. This is when you will be tested to see whether you are able to hold onto your faith.

It is extremely blessed and rare in the first place for an illness to be cured miraculously, but if you can only maintain your faith through continuous miracles, that is truly sad. The Bible mentions a miracle where Jesus Christ raises Lazarus from the dead after he was bound in strips of linen and had been placed in a tomb for four days. But even Lazarus passed away in due time. No one can live an eternal life in this world.

Numerous difficulties will occur, but you cannot live your life by solely depending on miracles. Sometimes you need wisdom to break through your obstacles. But even wisdom has its limits, and there may be times when you feel there is no way to overcome them. At such times, I want you to remember that this world was not created as a perfect place to begin with. This three-dimensional world was not created so that everyone, more than 100 million in Japan and over seven billion in the world, could fully achieve all their wishes.

In the other world, spirits of each dimension live together with those who have similar traits, but such a lifestyle does not provide enough of a variety of life experiences. That is why they are born into this world, to meet people from different realms or dimensions and refine their own lives in a mixed population. Humans reincarnate into this world for such a purpose.

Nonetheless, many things happen once you are born into this world. In the heavenly world, you may have had a spiritually high position and guided other beings in lower dimensions as an angel. But in this world, those who you used to guide in the heavenly world could have been born 10 or 20 years earlier than you, positioned as a superior in your company or a teacher at your school. Someone you used to guide in Heaven could even hold a rank that determines your future career in this world. A 22-year-old who is essentially an Angel of Light could be turned down at a job interview by a 40-year-old possessed by a devil because he or she feels the young interviewee is too straightforward and not a good fit for the company.

Our challenge for the infinite future— Bringing the world closer to the Kingdom of God

This world is irrational like that, and things do not quite go as we wish. Despite living in such a world, we must strive to replace what is the commonly accepted knowledge of this world with the commonly accepted knowledge of the Kingdom of God as much as we can. This is the significance of our missionary work.

We may clash over various issues in this world. We do not believe that everything will go smoothly only by following the laws and the systems created in this world. These rules may serve as a power to prevent the worst-case scenarios, but it is questionable whether they are choosing or producing the greatest good. So, our missionary work is also a continuous challenge for the infinite future, which always requires unlimited effort.

4

Transcend Hatred with Forgiving Love

✧   ✧   ✧

Even if you hate a person's deed,
Do not hate his or her essential being

When it comes to love, the kind of love you have realized, recognized and understood in this world is what really matters. Practicing a single concept of love is indeed very difficult. Earlier, I mentioned the idea of nurturing love, but I also teach forgiving love at Happy Science. Forgiving others is a very difficult thing to do, too. While loving others is difficult, forgiving is even more so.

You may not meet so many people who will tell you that they love you. Even if people love you, they may not tell you that. What is more, it is extremely rare for people to tell you that they forgive you. Those who steadily maintain a very religious state of mind may be able to say it, but not many will be able to say they forgive you at home, at school, or at work as they lead a mundane life.

Especially at work, mistakes cannot be forgiven; should one come up, its cause must of course be pursued. It is only natural for one to think, "Losses are unforgivable. We must always be profitable." You may sometimes point out others' mistakes or troubles at work and teach them where they went wrong. However, you need to know that reprimanding them to correct their mistakes and failures is not the same as hating them.

Even if you hate a person's deed, do not hate his or her essential being. Can you have such mindset? This is indeed a very difficult thing to do. A deed always produces a result. When someone does something, a result will follow. You will be tested to see if you are able to avoid harboring hatred toward a person after he or she produces a result that is unfavorable to you. For example, someone may prevent you from achieving your goal, become an obstacle at work, or interfere with your love affairs. When that happens, can you refrain from detesting that person? It is quite difficult not to despise that person. This feeling is instinctive, and some even believe it is inevitable.

Some countries teach their people to hate other countries

This chapter is based on a lecture I gave at the 2017 Celebration of the Lord's Descent which was broadcast via satellite to different parts of the world, including South Korea. Actually, we have a few dozen members in North Korea as well, though I do not know how North Korean people can become members. I am not sure if they were able to watch or listen to the lecture. Maybe they had some sort of secret way to watch or listen to it. Perhaps the information went through a different route. Anyway, we have believers there and I want to address them as well because people in the Korean Peninsula are often taught to despise others as a natural sentiment.

A Russian film director was able to enter North Korea and film a documentary about its current conditions with the permission and oversight of the North Korean authorities [a 2015 film by Vitaly Mansky, *Under the Sun*]. He actually had the cameras shooting in places where he was not allowed to film, like a scene where the authorities were giving directions to performers to make things look good. The footage was secretly brought out without being confiscated and the movie was screened.

In the movie, you can see that the common folk lack emotion, which is plainly visible. They have no expression and no one is smiling. They only act when they are instructed to do so. Otherwise, their faces are blank. The Russian director said that this was a typical feature of totalitarianism. Until a few decades ago, the Soviet Union was home to communism, and North Korea today is almost the same as a communist state.

The film shows elementary school teachers telling the students to hate the Japanese and landowners because they brought about the current state of North Koreans. Teachers also proclaim that the U.S. and South Korea started the Korean War, and that North Koreans must hate those countries because they plan to invade North Korea. However, the truth is actually the opposite. North Korea attacked South Korea first and advanced almost all the way to the southernmost tip of the Korean Peninsula, which is when the UN forces fought back. The battle came to a cease-fire with a border settled at the 38th parallel, but now there are signs of war again.

Thus, they are clearly educating their people to hate others.

In South Korea, on the other hand, Ms. Park Geun-hye, who was removed from presidential office, said that Koreans would continue to hold resentment for a thousand years for the era of former Japanese imperial rule. She made the statement while holding office as president. It is hard to imagine something like that happening in Japan. If the Japanese prime minister claimed that the Japanese would not forgive a foreign country for vile behavior for a thousand years, the Japanese mass media would claim the leader to be inhumane and question if that person was truly qualified to be prime minister. But in South Korea, this is possible. They must stop their hatred at some point, otherwise they will not progress any further.

Politicians in some countries try to justify their own actions by creating an enemy, but this is an extremely immature practice from a historical perspective. Just as the Nazis justified their actions by calling the Jews their enemy, such politicians tend to justify and rationalize their actions by casting blame on others as the enemy, but this is truly a frivolous tactic. I believe hatred must be overcome by love.

The opposite of love is jealousy, Which is the root of hatred

It is often said that the opposite of love is hatred, but I would rather say it is jealousy, which is the source of hatred. Jealousy makes people want to push others away or belittle them.

This was an enlightenment I attained in my younger years. I too had many feelings when I was young, such as the desire to compete, as well as superiority and inferiority complexes. But I realized as a young man that being envious of someone brighter or someone who attracted more attention out of an inferiority complex or jealousy would not make me happy at all. Instead of feeling envious, I made an effort to admire and praise people who could easily do things that I could not. Then, my views on life gradually changed.

If you are jealous and regard someone as your enemy, he or she will also tend to be hostile toward you, and the two of you will want to avoid each other. On the contrary, if you think that the person is nice, the feeling will somehow get across to that person and he or she will become your friend. Then, you can be part of a group of capable people, which will bring you many advantages. The other person, too, will be able to develop his or her character further.

5

What the World Needs is the Love of God

✧   ✧   ✧

The love of politicians should be
To make their people happy

What the world needs now is love. You might think that hatred is the opposite of love, but the reverse could also be jealousy. If jealousy invites competition and causes someone to hate another, it should be corrected.

Recently, for example, North Korea's nuclear development and missile launches have become a concern. I can understand they are doing their best to become equal with the U.S., but many of its people are emotionless and only do what they are told. It is a completely totalitarian and communist nation. In such systems, human lives are tools. They try to achieve outcomes by using a large number of people.

Democratic nations, on the other hand, aspire to serve their people. The people are an end, not a means. Ultimately, it is important for human beings to attain happiness, achieve self-realization, and grow by exercising their freedom. Ideally, countries should aim to achieve these goals.

From this, we can say that these two kinds of countries cannot be compared as equals. Every country is trying to promote its national defense by igniting the feeling of patriotism among its citizens, but we need to examine whether the country has a regime that makes its people happy.

On June 29, 2017, Chinese President Xi Jinping went to Hong Kong and said in a speech that while their "one country, two systems" policy would be maintained, any rebellion against authorities would not be allowed. But I assume that the people of Hong Kong who attended my lecture on May 22, 2011 will not accept that statement willingly. The citizens certainly have the right to pursue their own happiness.

I believe the love of politicians should be to make their people happy. This applies to Japan, too. I have the impression that the politicians today are preoccupied with love for themselves and love for their associates. I want to ask them if they truly love all the citizens of their country. If they do, they should consider doing things with a different perspective.

Practice the Love of God
In your daily words and actions

In the end, there is nothing, or no value, without the Love of God. Please know this. You may act based on love or say words of love, but if those actions and words, and their outcomes, do not contain the Love of God, they have absolutely no value. They are nothing. Please be aware of this.

Always ponder on what the Love of God is; as you do so, set your daily life right, deepen your state of mind and build on right actions every day. This is how I want you to live.

The one who Jesus called "Lord" and the one who Muhammad called "Allah" are the same Being. The Being who the Jews called "Elohim" is also this same Being, though Jews are now considered enemies of Christians and Muslims. This Being was born and is now alive on earth bearing the name, "El Cantare." My time left on earth may not be long, but I want to continue to preach the Laws to the very end, to their completion. Together, let us carry on making great efforts far into the future.

To Love is to Set Others Free, Believing the Goodness of Their Hearts

Start with giving love.

Set your daily goal on how you can give love to others.

What sort of love can you give to people and society?

Love is a blessing.

It is benevolence, an energy that tries to nurture others.

To love is to give the courage, the strength,

And the hope to live,

To the people we were meant to meet

During the course of our lives.

From this we can see that love is the Will of God,

Which nurtures and raises all living beings,

Helping them create a great harmony.

It is the will to help everything develop.

Once we are determined to start with "giving love,"

Our minds attune to God and shine with God's Light.

When we come to wish to nurture others,
Is when compassion as children of God
Has arisen in our hearts.

We need to know that love has two directions—
"Taking love" and "giving love."
Taking love is a love that has an attachment,
While giving love is free of any selfish desire
Or desire for self-preservation.

An obsessive love that wants to take hold of someone
And control his or her heart is not giving love.
No matter how much money you spend
Or how many things you give to someone,
If your aim is to bind them to you,
As if catching a bird and keeping it in a cage,
It is not giving love
But taking love, or love of attachment.

True love is a selfless love.
It is given for nothing,
Without expecting anything in return.

It helps another person grow and develop freely.

Love does not bind others,

But it sets them free,

Believing the goodness of their hearts.

Chapter THREE

The Gate to the Future

Use Your 30,000 Days of Life to Benefit the World

Lecture given on January 9, 2017
at Pacifico Yokohama, Kanagawa, Japan

1

Awaken and Set Up Your Goals in the Early Stages of Your Life

✧   ✧   ✧

Looking at your life from the viewpoint that Life is comprised of 30,000 days

This chapter is based on the lecture I gave on January 9, 2017, the Coming-of-Age Day in Japan,* on the theme of how we should lead our lives as human beings.

Those who are 20 years old now may believe they still have so many years ahead of them. The period between 10 and 20 probably felt quite long for them, and I, too, had the same feeling. From 20 to around 30, they will work with a single mind; they will have to tackle many challenges with all their might to become independent, working adults. This is the period when they learn to do their work as they are continually tested in their workplaces and accumulate various new experiences in their private lives as well. There will be times when they feel embarrassed or discouraged, and they need to consider what lessons they can grasp, so they can bounce back.

More people will get married starting around 30. After getting

---

* The Coming-of-Age Day is a Japanese holiday that is held annually on the second Monday of January. It is held to celebrate people who have newly entered adulthood. In Japan, the age of majority is 20 years old, and the local and prefectural governments hold ceremonies and give speeches to encourage and congratulate the new adults.

married, they will feel that time has sped up as if they are rolling down a steep slope. Being involved in various activities, they become extremely busy, wondering how they could spare time for themselves. But then before they know it, they reach what society calls retirement age and face a time limit in their careers. Most people will probably experience this; many in my generation are in their 60s and are now nearing their "final destination."

Nevertheless, some people consider this final destination to be their new starting point and continuously make efforts to try new things. Life for them is not over, and this is due to their attitude.

As I wrote in *The Laws of Mission* [(New York: IRH Press, 2017), the 23rd of the Laws Series], a life on earth is comprised of about 30,000 days; a 30,000-day-long life is actually longer than average. Those who are around 60 have already used up more than 20,000 days, and it is hard to tell if they can live another 10,000 days. Each day is like a grain of sand in an hourglass; a grain is falling every day.

Those who are around 20 may not really understand what I am saying. A lot of them probably believe they still have plenty of time and can spend it as they please. Furthermore, teenagers most likely expect their lives to last even longer into the future. However, the truth is, as I just said, that life on earth is limited; it will come to an end sooner than you think, before you actually achieve anything. I am sure many people in their twilight years will nod in agreement; they probably have faced such a reality in the latter half of their lives. This is why it is extremely important to be awakened in the early stages of your life.

Set up your aspirations first
And encourage yourself to achieve them

I strongly recommend those who have newly entered adulthood to set new resolutions for the future. Twenty years old is definitely not late. It is not too early, but not late. Setting one's aspirations and continually striving to achieve them from the early stage of life are surely not easy to do. To do so, you need to awaken to what you believe is your calling and, to find your proper path, you need to set out on a journey to discover yourself—through engaging in various studies, physical exercises, cultural activities, spending time with friends, encountering diverse values, or traveling abroad.

You may be spending your days in a common routine, such as working or raising a family, but it is extremely important for a young person to go a step further and find his or her true vocation, a job that makes one feel, "This is exactly what I was born to do." It is not easy to encounter a job that you want to continue throughout your life; the majority of people go through a process of trial and error, going on countless detours until they finally land on an appropriate path for them.

I am not saying this as a simple bystander. When I look back at how I was at 20, I would probably have resisted if I had been told to do the same job for the next 40 years. But while it is sometimes better not to know anything when it comes to what is waiting ahead of us, the things we have to do only increase with time.

In 1987, just before I turned 31, I gave a lecture, "The Principle of Love" [the second lecture of 1987, now included in aforementioned *The Science of Happiness*]. In that lecture, I said that we will start by entering a religious reformation phase for the first 10 years, and after that, we will start reformation in other fields including politics, education, and arts & culture. I have been working on the path to achieve these goals all along, but it has not been easy. It has taken tremendous time and energy.

Even if young people are told at this point now how much work they are expected to do, it may be hard to believe. So first, set up your goals. Have high aspirations and clarify what and how you want to achieve. Always have goals in your mind; desire so. Next, continually encourage yourself to achieve those goals. Eventually, a time will come when your intention clashes with reality. You will have to break through these walls while asking yourself why exactly you must achieve your goals regardless.

It is extremely difficult to make a mark in Japan Out of over 100 million people

There are over 120 million people living in Japan alone. The population is said to be decreasing, but even so, there are more than 100 million people. It is very hard to stand out in such a population. It is no simple task.

Happy Science has now also started work in the field of entertainment. Some of our members are appearing in various movies and TV dramas, but entertainment is actually a world of fierce competition. It is not easy to find a path to become a popular star. Looking only at the well-known stars, many people may wish they could be like them, but the fact is that only one in ten thousand, at best, can make it as a professional. Only one in a million can be a successful star that appears everywhere and is a household name. There is such a slim chance. Most of those wanting to become a star continuously go to auditions one after another, while supporting themselves by working part-time jobs. They might be successful in one out of fifty auditions, or even a hundred.

This does not only apply to those aiming to join the world of entertainment; the same goes for those aiming to become novelists. For example, one Akutagawa Prize[*] winner wrote a novel based on her actual experience working in a convenience store, but she still continues working there even after having won the award because she was told by the publisher that she needed to continue working there to support herself. It is indeed true that you cannot make a living from just winning one award; you have only taken your first step on the path to success, and it is still uncertain whether you can write a second or a third title to become a professional writer. This is how tough reality is.

---

[*] The Akutagawa Prize is a prestigious Japanese literary award presented semi-annually to new and recent writers. It is named after a prominent Japanese novelist, Ryunosuke Akutagawa [1892 – 1927].

Decades ago, many people, regardless of whether they were from cities or the provinces, believed they were assuredly on the route to success as long as they achieved high academic standing, studied hard from elementary school and steadily raised their academic performance to get into elite schools. But the reality is unfortunately much tougher now.

Around the time of the Koizumi administration* in the 2000s in Japan, the expressions "winners in life" and "losers in life" were widely used, but not anymore. That is because we have entered an era when there are no winners in life. There are very few, if any. In this era, those who appear to be winners are immediately shot down, leaving no winners. A strong force is at work to drag people down to average or below average, and it is becoming an era when only subpar people can swagger around in society. This is truly a troublesome situation.

---

* The Koizumi administration lasted five years from April 2001 to September 2006, when Junichiro Koizumi was in office as the prime minister of Japan.

2

Happy Science Has
The Power to Foresee the Future

✧　✧　✧

The development of 30-plus years of Happy Science,
And our future visions

Japan's economic bubble began to burst in 1990, but around that time, Japan was the most competitive country in the world. Happy Science was entering its fourth year of activities since its founding, and was doing quite well. While the Japanese society was experiencing economic trouble, Happy Science was very active and charging ahead at full speed without giving it any thought.

Then in the first half of 1990s, various weekly magazines began to criticize us, saying something like, "Happy Science has no idea how much society is suffering after the bubble burst." I was focusing on my work nonetheless because we had just started with our activities and had a bright future ahead of us. I gave lectures at Tokyo Dome for five consecutive years from 1991 to 1995. But upon seeing the enormous gap between what was on the front pages of newspapers and the activities of Happy Science, people began to see us in a negative light. There was an intense storm of jealousy, and evil religious groups were running rampant, too. I felt

I bore some responsibility for that, and decided to spend more time strengthening the foundation of our organization in a mature way, without being too provocative.

In particular, 1995 was the year when the Japanese religious group Aum Shinrikyo became the target of social blame after its sarin attack in Tokyo subway stations. We said we were a completely different religion and irrelevant to the incident; rather, we did all we could to help resolve the issue. Despite that, society treated all new religious groups the same, saying that they were either all good or all bad.

Given that, I thought we had to bear some responsibility for the public's impression of religion, so we decided to tack. I cut back on the number of large public lectures, while on the other hand, focused on constructing our own temples and local branches throughout Japan and the world, building up internal resources by training personnel, and on producing software for educational and missionary work. For a decade or so, we carried out our activities as we underplayed our strength.

Then, we rebounded. We restarted passionate missionary work in Japan while promoting overseas missionary work. In addition, we launched political activities and intensified our efforts in the field of education. After spending 10 years or so quietly building up our strength, we began to move again to influence society. During those years, many of our rivals disappeared. In this sense, it was a wise strategy.

It is not easy to keep winning in society, as if running on a single railroad track. Ironically, it is when you are enjoying a good reputation, that you are often in tough times, and when you are not attracting any attention from society, you are in fact making progress. It is difficult to find the right balance.

The same is probably true with your work. It is when you are getting recognition and doing well that you might find many enemies around you, staring at you coldly. When you are very satisfied with the achievements of your company is when your enemies sometimes gradually and silently approach you, or something happens to damage the environment of your industry. In this way, things can turn out to become the exact opposite in many situations, so we always need to be wary.

In 2017, Happy Science marked the 31st anniversary of its founding. During this time, we persisted in our efforts to build up what we had to, and withstood what needed to be endured while keeping a low profile, believing that these years of continuous activity would qualify us to receive "civil rights." We single-heartedly aimed to achieve our goals during this entire time. When I look at the whole world, however, there is still a lot of work that requires our efforts, although unfortunately, much is still beyond what we are currently capable of doing.

The time has now come to accelerate our activities again. This is why I gave a large public lecture at Tokyo Dome with the title, "The Choice of Humankind" on August 2, 2017 [the transcript of the lecture was translated and edited as Chapter Six in this book]. It had been many years since the last time I gave one there.

It is about time to promote our activities with all our heart and soul.

Saving energy takes efforts, too. We get older while saving our energy, which is not good. Unless we train our bodies, they will eventually get weak and decline. This is a serious matter. It will be too late once we become weak, so we must step on the gas now. Otherwise, we will not be able to fulfill our true mission.

Taking the time to create and nurture believers

In 2017, I published *The Laws of Mission*. Judging from the title, it might not seem like the kind of book that will become a bestseller. Many people may actually think that way and say, "There is no way that such a book will sell well. We can't even recommend people to read it." I understand this would be the general reaction. However, Happy Science *will* make it a bestseller regardless. Anyone can make a bestseller with a book that seems like it would be a bestseller, but our work is to do so with a book that does not seem like it would be a bestseller. We are determined to make *The Laws of Mission* the year's bestseller, as we always do.

Happy Science has been producing a succession of bestsellers for around 26 years now. I feel sorry for other publishers who might be envious, wondering how we are able to create a system that can produce bestsellers every year. Books, in general, are liked by some, but not by others. Some people may have a favorite author, but they do not necessarily like all of his or her works, and it is not easy for an author to have ardent and loyal fans.

Happy Science has indeed such a readership. It is not easy to foster people to become believers like ours, who always bounce back no matter how many times they are pushed down. It takes 30 years to build up such people. It is similar to the process of making mochi, or rice cake, for the New Year;* pounding the rice many times into a smooth paste takes time, so it cannot be done instantly. In the same way, people need to go through happy times as well as unfortunate ones, experiencing both favorable and unfavorable winds in order to become true believers.

Happy Science can confidently take a firm stand against the mass media, and this is also thankfully due to the hard work of those who became our strong believers over time. All sorts of things have happened in these 30 years, but they have persistently followed me. I am impressed and deeply appreciative of them.

The reason why I look young and ageless

Those who were as young as me when we started out have seemingly aged more than I have. Sometimes I cannot even recognize them. To think that they have worked so hard for so long brings tears to my eyes. Day after day, I am moved by their hard work.

Many of our believers have aged and so have I. Still, I probably appear a bit more youthful. It is a matter of attitude—I believe I am

*It is a Japanese tradition to pound the rice to make mochi for the New Year.

still at the halfway mark. I have to complete the return leg of the marathon, which is just as long as the distance I have come, so I am far from finished. I cannot end the race yet; rather, I believe the real work starts now.

While we were still a small group, the general public did not pay very much attention to us, even when we made shocking remarks. They did not take what we said very seriously. However, once we grew to a certain level and people began to acknowledge us, they started to listen to us very seriously instead of getting offended, even when we voiced our opinions very harshly. This really is a strange phenomenon, but to win the trust of the general public, we needed to persevere through all that time and accumulate sufficient achievements.

The forecast of the world economy and politics: Violent fluctuations

We advertised this lecture given at Pacifico Yokohama and its national broadcast, which this chapter is based on, in the Japanese newspapers. Apparently, it attracted the interest of some particular people. On the morning of the day before my lecture, I sensed the presence of some ikiryos, or the combination of a person's strong thoughts and his or her guardian spirit. I was surprised to be visited so early in the day, on the New Year. There was the ikiryo of Japanese Prime Minister Abe, followed by the ikiryo of Minister of Defense

Tomomi Inada [at the time of the lecture]. They said, "Please don't scold us at tomorrow's lecture." They came to me with such a request.

In my lecture at the end of 2016 ["The Way to the Truth" given on December 7, 2016, included in *The Decision Toward Prosperity* (Tokyo: HS Press, 2017)], I candidly pointed out the problems of the Abe administration and it seemed my remarks struck home. So, in this chapter, I will not go too deeply into that.

I know they are working hard. They are trying hard to produce positive results through playing golf with important people at the end and the beginning of the year. I, personally, cannot spend my time like that; I am afraid our members would be disappointed if they saw me playing golf. Just celebrating the New Year in a traditional way might be accepted, but playing golf would be too much. From the New Year, Mr. Abe enjoyed golf in Chigasaki City, Kanagawa Prefecture near Tokyo; he may have been intending to build up his physical strength before visiting Russia, but I cannot even think of doing that. He may indeed have a lot of stamina.

Some of my readers may expect me to share my views on current events or what should be done on the national level, or on a macro scale. For example, many may want to know about market fluctuations because they want to make a profit. They might ask, "How much will market prices be affected with the rise of the Trump administration? How much will stock prices rise? When will prices rise and when will they fall? I can gain a lot if you show me clearly on a chart. I am willing to donate half of my gains." But it is inappropriate for me to say anything about the subject.

It would be considered cheating if I did.

What I *can* say is that we will see a lot of violent fluctuations, with many ups and downs, in 2017 and beyond. Some will win, while others will lose. If you continue betting on stocks, you will most probably lose. You can try after good consideration, but it will be difficult to keep winning because even if stock prices might rise for some time, they will eventually fall.

The same kind of violent fluctuations may well be observed in politics. There will be times when things appear to be going well, times when things get suddenly worse, times when there will be a potential crisis, and times when problems get solved unexpectedly. All sorts of things can and will most likely happen.

The strength of the Happiness Realization Party: The ability to foresee the future

Public support for the Happiness Realization Party remains at a stable level and there may not be any major changes for the time being. Nevertheless, we just have to keep trying to make a breakthrough anywhere we can; just as in a baseball game, we will continuously go after the pitches, hoping that one will become an infield hit. We must increase our pace to gain popularity very soon.

This being said, our influence is steadily expanding. For example, in December 2016, Vice Party Leader Sakurako Jimmu of the Happiness Realization Party and Director General Kazuhiro

Takegawa of the Happy Science International Public Relations Division [at the time of this lecture] went to Russia to attend an international forum [a Japan-Russia forum commemorating the 60th anniversary of the re-establishment of diplomatic relations between Japan and Russia, held at the Moscow State Institute of International Relations (MGIMO)]. In that forum, the Happiness Realization Party was treated as the most welcomed Japanese guest among other Japanese guests.

When Vice Party Leader Jimmu confidently laid out our policies by saying, "Let's create an economic exchange by connecting the Trans-Siberian Railway to Japan," the Russian side showed full agreement. They even commented that Russia and Japan could cooperate on the nuclear issue of North Korea. It was as though they already knew our opinions.

Their intelligence network is incredible. It is not just the Democratic Party in the U.S. who is being spied on by the Russian intelligence service; opinions released by Happy Science in Japanese also reach various destinations that very same day. The scope of our influence is far greater than what the Japanese mass media can imagine. It now extends to powerful places, to the world's core players. Happy Science members can be confident about this point. It means Happy Science activities are having a global influence.

When Prime Minister Abe was desperately seeking a way to create a channel to President Trump of the Republican Party, Happy Science was already active in supporting Mr. Trump in the U.S. I even visited Trump Tower before Prime Minister Abe did.

When I went to the U.S. to give the lecture, "Freedom, Justice, and Happiness," on October 2, 2016, I also visited Trump Tower. It was long before Mr. Abe did. This is what you call foresight.

It is very important to be able to see ahead. This ability is crucial in running a business, leading a country, or launching an educational project. It is particularly important for those in management, who support the livelihoods of many employees. There would be big problems if these people misread current international relations or large-scale trends.

The foolishness of generalizing one case

According to what I have heard, the Japanese government is now encouraging its people to end work by 3 pm on Fridays and spend their money on recreation. In this way, they expect the economy to get better and the people to become happier. I am surprised by the fact that there is a country on this globe that adopts such a policy. What is more, the government even encourages workers and their families to enjoy themselves in the casinos that are to be built. This is truly frightening; it sends shivers down my spine.

Earlier, I said Japan was the most competitive country in the world in 1990. In those times, too, many people commented that it was the time for research and resorts, that it was time to develop many resort areas and think about how to enjoy themselves. The co-founder of Sony, Mr. Akio Morita, traveled around the U.S. and

Europe and found that the Japanese worked more hours compared to workers in Western countries. He thought the Japanese should spend more time on recreational activities, and encouraged people to take vacations. Soon after that, however, the Japanese economy plunged into a great recession.

I get a similar sense now. While I feel that Japan's economy has been stagnant for such a long period of time and that this is dangerous, some leaders are saying, "Let's shift toward recreation and have fun. Spend more money and boost our economy through recreational activities." I am concerned and anxious about this.

Recently, I have the feeling that there are too many national holidays, though this may only be my biased impression. Happy Science appreciates when the nation has three-day weekends because we can take that opportunity to provide more events during those weekends; I am truly grateful for having more chances to work. But Japanese employees seem to be working less and less. This is my impression. Japan has more national holidays than the U.S. does. I feel that this is a problem and I am very concerned about it. I feel that the Japanese people need to work a little more.

A worker at a Japanese major advertising company died recently from overwork, and this became a social issue. Since then, there has been strong opinion against overwork, and people are saying they should work less. However, if this goes too far, unemployment could increase. Therefore, we need to think carefully and view things in a more balanced way. It is not good to generalize one case.

How we should view and judge
The one-sided information of the mass media

One thing we need to bear in mind when looking at things in a balanced way is that some mass media—maybe more than half of them—have a tendency to magnify small matters and downplay big ones. They have a habit of writing small articles about powerful or influential events while enlarging insignificant events. This is something to be careful about.

For example, there were Japanese news reports of local residents in the Hokuriku area [region west of Tokyo on the Sea of Japan] spotting an increased number of deer, or that an Asian black bear was seen wandering through a hot springs resort. And even a photo of a drooling panda was featured in the news. My wife Shio Okawa published a book, *Panda-gaku Nyumon* [literally, "Introduction to 'Learning from Panda'" (Tokyo: Happy Science, 2016)], so she was delighted to see that news item and stated, "Pandas can make the news just by drooling. What a life."

Newspapers write about such trifle events, but often neglect very important matters. This causes these crucial events to proceed quietly under the radar until they become so serious that they suddenly burst into the spotlight. So, we could easily overlook important issues in their early stages. The mass media may believe that highlighting rare events will make them stand out, while covering major stories will make them look as if they are just following or aligning themselves with public opinion. But they need to watch things more carefully.

Japan's current economic, political, and diplomatic policies are at such a low level that I do not have much to say; I feel there is no point in saying anything. Such things have already reached the level where there is no fundamental solution. It cannot be helped because the people in government are unable to understand what I am saying. But all things will eventually pass. I will, of course, continue to speak out or make occasional comments whenever necessary, but we must first do whatever we can by ourselves.

I am not sure how many days you have remaining in your life, but you must value each and every day. Thirty thousand days will be over before you know it. Time flies by, so it is extremely important to move forward in some way, even if it is just one step, in a direction that benefits humankind or the people of future generations as much as possible; please make each day of your life like this.

3

The Keys to Open the Gate to the Future

✧　　✧　　✧

Do not agree with the thoughts and logic that would Lead individuals and society toward degradation

What are the kinds of attitudes we need to keep in mind to open the gate to the future? One is to stay away from becoming dependent on large-scale macro policies, or the policies of a big government. Government policies may eventually work to make people's lives more or less easier, but a country whose government has to raise the minimum wage of its citizens is not a good country. This is not good because it means freedom is dead; you could say that in such a country, the spirit of capitalism is nearly dead and democracy is losing its brilliance. This country is entering such an era.

The best part of popular democracy is that it can protect fundamental human rights, but as people try to protect those fundamental human rights, the whole country could gradually become poor. There is such a trend in Japan and it is quite difficult to stop. The Bank of Japan had set negative interest rates, and now we are seeing an era of ultra-low interest rates, generating almost no interest on your savings in a bank. You can no longer expect to become rich by simply depositing your money in a bank and letting it earn interest, nor will you be able to gain enough capital to invest in a large business. It is obvious that we are living in such times.

Nevertheless, I want to stress that even if your savings do not earn interest, this does not mean you should spend your money extravagantly. Rather, each and every person needs to look carefully to see if a product is truly necessary when deciding to purchase it. If you are manipulated by government strategies and continue to spend your money, as an individual or as a company, then you will definitely end up in great trouble.

Japan is gradually moving toward a welfare nation like the Northern European countries, whether it is the Democratic Party of Japan or the Liberal Democratic Party in power. But which of those countries is a good example for Japan? Being able to give out Nobel prizes might be a good thing, but that is not the kind of country Japan should simulate.

Then, what should Japan aim for now? I believe Japan should boost its global competitiveness and educational capabilities to the next level, express its political and economic opinions, and gain the strength to lead the world.

I want each and every person to think very carefully so as not to head toward degradation, either as an individual or as a society. Your savings account might earn very little interest, almost none, but this definitely does not mean you should spend your money nonchalantly and waste it. This needs to be noted. Although you may have to pay for your savings account due to the negative interest rate policy, it is still better to save than to spend it all. It would be like a maintenance fee to secure your money in a bank, like having security companies protect you. If you see it in that way, perhaps you will agree to pay some fees.

Wasting money is indeed a silly behavior; the money you gained through hard work is so precious that you must spend it on what is truly important for your own future and the future of the world. Develop the habit of prioritizing how you spend your money. Please keep this in mind. This is one point I have to make. To put it differently, do not easily agree with the thoughts that would lead people and the world toward degradation.

Strive tenaciously throughout your life, Both in your work and at home

There is another point I have to make. In the coming years, various countries will come into the spotlight and it may appear as if a superpower may emerge among them. At such times, Japan needs to have the power of tenacity. For the past 20 to 25 years, Japan has seemingly been slowly receding, but it does not need any special abilities or discoveries to change the tide. It is rather important to acquire the power to persevere once again. Every citizen must have the tenacious power to be resilient and continue making efforts.

The problem is that many people get scared and give up. In 1990, there were signs that Japan would become the number one economic power in the world, but it got scared and retreated.

That was how I saw Japan at that time. It should have kept going, set various goals to actually become the world leader, and evolved one step further. But there was no one who could share the vision. That was the major reason why Japan retreated.

It is rather strange that the Japanese people are frustrated about the fact that Japan is gradually falling behind when in fact it now has fewer working days and hours than America. I want each citizen to think about putting more effort into creating good habits and doing good work based on them. This is a matter of enthusiasm rather than talent. Enthusiasm is worthless unless it is backed by effort, and effort must be made to push you forward to develop new and good habits. It is essential that, as a result of this, you accomplish good work by giving tenacious efforts that runs throughout your life.

Of course, your current work that generates income is very valuable. In addition, think of how you can make tenacious efforts at home. It is also important for Happy Science members to participate regularly in the various activities we carry out, although you might not be able to attend all of them. I wish that the lives of our members improve, especially the devoted ones who make our events a priority, even on their days off or national holidays. As they seriously study the Truth, I hope they will find something meaningful that makes them want to keep at it throughout their lives.

4

What Will Happen to You in the Future, After Your Death?

✧　　✧　　✧

The other world awaits us after death

In some respect, missionary work in religion may resemble sales or marketing work in a company, but if you give up on it based on such a belief, that is the end of it. Missionary work of religion is not something that you are selling for money. It is by no means a sales transaction, but far deeper than that—it is something that involves wisdom of life. The aforementioned *The Laws of Mission* describes this from various angles. It may not be easy to understand everything right away, but let me put it simply here.

If you view things according to the current cultural climate of Japan based on its trends in education, society, and the mass media, for example, you will most likely be led to a world of total ignorance, in other words, a world of materialistic atheism or agnosticism. However, what will happen as the result of this?

People will leave this world after 30,000 days of life. But probably more than half of the people who are so-called "intellectuals" believe this world is all that exists and see humans as a kind of machine. Many people may think, "There is no such thing as the mind or soul. It's just the workings of the brain. The brain thinks and makes decisions, so we cannot do anything when the brain is damaged. Therefore, being in a vegetative state is the same as being dead." However, this is absolutely wrong.

There is another world after we die. The other world truly exists. I guarantee you 100 percent that it exists. If, after death, you discover that this is not true, then come and complain to me. I will teach you that the other world does exist.

People have a life in the other world even after they die. The other world exists even for those who have received a materialist education and become an atheist, who have come to believe there is no Buddha, God, angels or bodhisattvas, and that everything ends with death.

The knowledge about Heaven and Hell Will change our way of life

Upon returning to the other world, some fall straight down to Hell. Those who influenced others negatively or who led others in the wrong direction are destined to go there. There are different kinds of Hell, and I can tell you all about them, if and when necessary.

Those who were not as bad, or who simply did not really know anything about the other world, will first go to some kind of transit area. Those who have no idea about where they should go will be in between this world and the other for the time being. Those gathering in this transit area all wonder, "There is no such thing as the other world. I am dead and my body is gone, but I'm still here. Why? Who am I? Where am I? What is this place?"

There are spirits who take the role of teaching them and sort out, little by little, to determine their destinations in the other world. With such guidance, some will understand the situation and move on to Heaven, while others will move on to Hell to undergo spiritual training. Whether it is in the near or distant future, this certainly lies ahead for each one of you and for the people you know.

In an effort to prove that, I have been conducting spiritual messages and readings in public, which have now exceeded 700 sessions [as of November 2017]. Even I think giving this many sessions is not an easy thing to do. People could make up one or two stories, but no one would be able to make up 700 different spiritual messages. There is no way anyone can do such a thing. *Manga* artists, or cartoonists, would not be able to come up with so many different stories, either. That is only natural. I can do this because they are true.

It is tremendously important to teach people the existence of the other world because prior knowledge will determine their way of life, or their lifestyle, in this world. If you know that the other world exists, you can decide, in advance, how you ought to live in this world, and you can prepare for life after death. You can find your own answer as to how you can lead a life of no regrets in the time you have until you die. Once you know what awaits you in the afterlife, you can work backward and decide how to live the rest of your life, as well as save others who are lost.

The power of the Truth opens up a path of salvation For your ancestors and relatives who are lost

In reality, countless souls are lost in the other world; they do not know that they are dead, even after 50 years. There are many such souls at the Yasukuni Shrine in Japan, for example. Among the Japanese soldiers who lost their lives in World War II, some came all the way to Yasukuni Shrine after death, from Okinawa or Leyte in the Philippines, but since they had no knowledge about the other world while they were alive, they did not know what to do next. As a result, they still wander around there.

The Shinto priests there do not seem to have the power to send these souls to the other world, which is troublesome. For these souls to be saved, their bereaved families must attain a certain level of enlightenment. For the souls who are still wandering even after 50 or 70 years after death, the path to salvation will finally open when their family members and relatives awaken to and gain knowledge of the Truth.

Carry out your missionary activities To save the souls of many people

The road to missionary work is the road to save many people. It is valuable work to truly save the souls of many; more valuable than the worldly practice of love or salvation work. Happy Science is carrying out many different activities in this world to promote our missionary work, but we are well aware of the difference between what we do as expedient means and what we must essentially do. I hope our members will understand various instructions and policies given by Happy Science based on this understanding.

For instance, we released our new movie, *The World We Live In* [executive producer Ryuho Okawa], in May 2017. It is probably the best movie we have produced so far. It is a spiritual movie that will help you understand the Truth, as you are entertained. I hope you will have a chance to watch it. Recent trends have shown that popular films in Japan draw much attention and are widely accepted overseas as well, which is why we created such a movie that will help to spread the Truth. We are aiming to get lots of viewers in Japan and hope to gain the opportunity to get many viewers outside Japan, too.

We are now living in an age in which everyone, without exception, can restart his or her life to head in a good direction, toward the heavenly world, by gaining the knowledge of the true world. People living today are witnessing the moment when the gate to the future of new hope is about to open. Please be aware of this and push open this gate to the future with your own strength.

Have a Strong Conviction on Wealth

Many people do not realize
That what is unfolding before their very eyes
Is what they, themselves, have truly desired.

What they think on the superficial consciousness
Is different from what they repeatedly think
In the depths of their minds, or in the subconscious.
That is why they feel, "This is not what I wanted!"

However, oftentimes,
People around them will see and think,
"Their thoughts have come true, that's all."

People may say,
"I want to make more money. I want to be rich."
But when you observe them,
Many of them do not seem to behave that way.
You will doubt whether they truly want
To be rich and affluent

Because there is a disparity between what they wish for
And what they actually say and do.

If you want to be rich,
Do not hate wealth.
Do not hate to be affluent.
Do not regard success as a bad thing.

Although you may say you want to be rich,
If you reject success in the depths of your heart,
Something will block your way,
Which you could later use as an excuse for your failure,
Eventually keeping you from becoming rich.

For example,
Just when you think your business is on track for success,
Something happens to obstruct your way,
Such as you falling ill or having an accident,
Or an obstacle or a rival appearing.
It happens because deep in your heart,
You do not wish for your business to go well.

Your thoughts are not fully focused on success.

Your conviction is weak.
You do not fully believe that thoughts have actual power.
This is something
That cannot be easily and fully understood.
That is why, when you wish for something,
You hold a subtle thought, and less often a firm belief.

Chapter FOUR

The World Religion of Japanese Origin will Save the Earth

*Building up a Nation that will Serve
to Eliminate All Conflicts from This Planet*

Lecture given on January 16, 2011
at Tokyo Shoshinkan, Tokyo, Japan

1

The Fundamental Spirit of
A Nation Stems from Religion

✧   ✧   ✧

The age of love and mercy has arrived

In this chapter, I would like to expound the contents of the 16th book of my Laws Series, *The Laws of Salvation* [Tokyo: Happy Science, 2012]. The book was published in Japanese in 2011, a year that marked a milestone for Happy Science; the 30th anniversary of my attaining Great Enlightenment in 1981, the 25th anniversary of the start of our activities in 1986, and the 20th anniversary of our official registration as a religious legal body in 1991. Like bamboo that grows taller by creating joints at certain interval, I want to use this milestone as a rung to step up further and work hard to make Happy Science grow to the next level.

In the preface of *The Laws of Salvation*, I described my feeling after reaching the 30th anniversary of my Great Enlightenment. To speak directly, I declared myself as a savior. I wrote, "The Savior has appeared again, in Japan, 2,500 years after he passed away as Buddha. Japanese people have yet to believe in me despite my having taught so many Laws. This is truly deplorable. The Rebirth of Buddha also signifies the Second Coming of Christ. I want to save the Earth from its crises and open the way for the upcoming Space Age. The arrival of the age of mercy and love has again been declared."

Additionally, the afterword of the book starts off with the sentence, "Now, a new world religion is about to rise from Japan." Near the end, it says, "More simply, El Cantare gave birth to world religions including Buddhism, Christianity and Islam." The words were written as simple statements, but the truth is that the book was a calm challenge that I posed to the world, 30 years since my Great Enlightenment.

Is a nation that denies religion allowed to prosper?

The Laws of Salvation very clearly indicates the reason why Happy Science exists and what its aims are, among the many other religions in the world. These fundamental statements are backed by considerable determination. We have been carrying out various activities for more than 35 years now, but I feel we have not yet managed to radically change the current and commonly accepted knowledge prevalent in Japan. My impression is that although Happy Science is accepted as one of the influential religions in Japan, we have only remained at that level. We need to break out and aim for the next level.

Here are essential questions I ask the Japanese people. "Are Japanese people truly civilized? Do they possess a high level of cultural capital? Does the Japanese culture or civilization really deserve to be accepted as it is? Does it have a promising future?" To be more specific, I am questioning whether a country where people who deny religion are the majority, a nation that does not respect or value religion, should continuously be allowed to grow and prosper the way it has been.

To put this differently, Japan's status quo is no different from a world of animals. All that matters for animals is to get their daily food to sustain their lives. However, that is not enough for human beings. Humans must perceive unseen values and find meaning in living for the sake of those values. Otherwise, they do not satisfy the basic reason for being human. This is what I have been repeatedly teaching.

Establishing a spiritual backbone In "a drifting country" Japan

When doing missionary work overseas, I sense that Japan stands on shaky and uncertain ground. The footing is unsure as though we are standing on a muddy surface. Japan's spiritual foundation is weak and very fragile; there is very little spiritual backbone. Japan is literally a drifting country. I sometimes wonder if, in fact, the Japanese islands are really connected to the earthen base deep under the sea, or they are just floating on the surface of the ocean like jellyfish.

This lack of spiritual backbone is affecting Japan's politics, foreign diplomacy, and many other areas. Its education system is also affected; children learn truly deplorable values at schools. As a result, classes and education are falling apart especially in public schools, giving way to problems such as bullying. Children raised by adults who have lost respect for their country will have difficulty finding the true meaning of life, fulfilling work, or confidence in their future.

I want to establish a strong backbone in Japan, a jellyfish-like country. I have repeatedly said this in the past. This backbone is the basic spirit that a nation should have. It is based on morality, and the root of morality is religion. Religion is superior to philosophy.

There is no future for people Who cannot assert what is right

Unless religion is firmly rooted, a country would be spineless, just like how Japan is right now. Currently, Japan is in constant disorder. Whether being the second or third in the world in terms of GDP is of minor importance. What is deplorable is that a nation ranking near the top among nearly 200 countries in the world is unable to deliver any message with spiritual value, give clear opinions, or provide leadership for the world. Japanese people must be more aware of this fact.

Japanese people are not bearing the responsibility appropriate to their global standing. They should be ashamed of that. I have a strong feeling like this welling up from within. Japan should not remain adrift. What it needs to do now is to set up a firm spiritual foundation. Japan needs a spiritual backbone. To do this, we must be able to confidently refute those who view religion lightly or make fun of it. This is how Japan should be. Its people must be able to assert what is right, otherwise there will be no future for them.

2

Experience the Moments When You Feel The Light and Rebuild Your Life

✧　✧　✧

As spiritual beings, Humans inhabit physical bodies to live on earth

Chapter 1 of *The Laws of Salvation*, titled "The Recommendation of Religion," talks about the basic Truths that everyone should know. They are second nature to Happy Science believers because I have taught them so many times.

The first Truth is, "Humans are essentially spiritual beings and, as spiritual beings, they inhabit physical bodies to live on earth." This Truth is not taught in school education, whether at the elementary school, junior or senior high school, or college level, neither is it taught as a norm in society. In fact, people who are recognized as the elite in society rather have a tendency to say the complete opposite. They consider denying this Truth as being correct and proof of being intelligent. This is very unfortunate.

Of course, I am well aware that people have the rights to freedom of thought, freedom of speech, freedom of expression, and the freedom of the press. I believe it is a good thing to have many different opinions, expressions, and ideas. However, it is a disgrace for humans to lack the wisdom to distinguish between facts and untruths.

Although everyone is free to speak their minds, there are certain hard facts. For example, hydrogen [H] and oxygen [O] combine to become water [H_2O], not oil. You could talk about the freedom of speech, but when someone says that the combination of hydrogen and oxygen produces oil, and that his or her ideas should be accepted as part of the freedom of speech, there is something wrong. It is fine to express hundreds of thoughts on unknown matters, but the fact that the bond of hydrogen and oxygen produces water is made clear by the chemical formula, H_2O. In cases like this, the freedom of speech does not mean to insist, "oil is produced, not water."

I am saying the same thing about spiritual truths. Although it is fine to have various opinions, the truths do exist. There are truths in life. Those who teach or study untruths, or act in ways that go against the truths will eventually experience some kind of reaction, either during or after their lives. This reaction will occur not only on the individual, but also to the organization, society, country or world in which these people are members.

The final judgment on the personal level
That each of you will face after death

Whatever one may think or say, my accumulated research over the past 35-plus years shows 100 percent that another world exists after death. If you believe that you are only your physical body, you are undoubtedly mistaken. A doctor, who has graduated from a prestigious medical university, may say, "Once you die, your life is over," but what is wrong is wrong. We must clearly assert what is wrong from the standpoint of human dignity as wrong.

What exists indeed exists. In a few years or maybe decades, everyone will experience this for themselves without exception, so I hope you remember my words. If you find even one thing wrong with what I teach, come and complain to me as a spirit. So far, not a single one has come and complained. In fact, spirits usually come to me and say, "Everything was exactly how you taught. I'm glad I knew this beforehand." They all say this.

The reality is that those who did not learn the Truth are in such a state of confusion, unaware of where to go, that they would not be able to come to me to begin with. Nonetheless, I want people to know that there is a world where worldly knowledge or intelligence, social ranking, family standing, the fame of one's business, or the difference between man and woman, are totally irrelevant.

In this world, you may have different backgrounds and do various kinds of work, but each of you will eventually face death and depart for the other world. What you can take back with you at that time is only your mind, and you will be tested as to whether your mind has the right faith. In other words, you will undoubtedly be judged as to whether you lived your life with faith in God and Buddha, or whether you lived your life being swayed by the values of the devils in Hell that are actively trying to hinder people's faith in God and Buddha. This is the final judgment for you on the personal level.

The final judgment comes not only to individuals, but also to organizations, societies and nations. In short, the future can change in whichever direction depending on the nature of faith those organizations, societies, and nations hold. I strongly believe so.

Japan's religious situation is quite different From the international norm

I teach the Laws differently overseas than in Japan, even when I speak on the same topic. This is because the level of faith is different among nations. Of course, it may partly be due to the fact that people in countries not as developed as Japan respect it as a developed nation, so they pay close attention to what a Japanese person has to say. Even so, people with spiritual understanding in religious nations take in my teachings very naturally.

For example, in Uganda, Africa, my English lectures were broadcast on national TV every week, and so was our movie, *The Rebirth of Buddha* [executive producer Ryuho Okawa, released in 2009]. In Nepal too, my English lectures were broadcast on national

TV, and in Mumbai, India, part of my lecture was shown with Hindi subtitles. This is very unlikely to happen on Japanese TV.

In Japan, reporting on matters relating to religion in a positive way, or cooperating with spreading the teachings of a specific religion, is considered unethical by the mass media [recently, however, some of the local TV stations have started broadcasting my public lectures]. This means the people in Japan are having their religious choices being made for them, the choice of whether they stand by God and Buddha, or with devils, since not standing by God and Buddha automatically means that they are standing with devils. This means they are making efforts to turn this world into Hell.

The same applies to school education. For example, the Japanese education system denies the ancient Japanese mythologies, including *Kojiki* [Records of Ancient Matters] and *Nihon Shoki* [Chronicles of Japan]. They are not mentioned in school textbooks. Classes may cover some traditional religions besides Japanese Shinto, but merely as interesting archeological facts, rather than delving into their teachings. As a result, people do not naturally awaken to religious faith through any school education unless they attend private Christian schools and the like.

Furthermore, if people study religion at universities, they are even more likely to deny religious faith. Religious studies in Japanese universities are not based on any understanding of faith; they try to omit any subjectivity and only focus on analyzing religion for research. It is not very different from the process where medical students dissect human cadavers and study body parts. No one can answer "what is right" or "what is good and what is bad," so religious studies in universities are completely useless.

Humans are children of God and Buddha, And are endowed with a part of His Light

Japan came to be the way it is now most probably due to its defeat in World War II. As a result of its loss, Japan made the great shift toward denying faith. However, Japan needs to wake up from this nightmare very soon and regain its true power. Unless Japanese people regain the power of faith, they cannot harbor spiritual power in their bodies, nor can they have power that emerges from within. I want you to consider deeply which view of life serves you better; the view that humans are children of God and Buddha, who are endowed with a part of His Will and Light, or the view that humans were just formed by coincidence, no different from pieces of clay or machinery.

Nowadays, the Japanese society encourages people to hold views of life that would make them a meaningless existence. To counter this trend, I have been criticizing Japan's current education system and the mass media for contributing to this situation, but honestly, the world of religion is also utterly corrupt. There are many religions in Japan, but the majority of them are not fulfilling their true mission. Rather, a lot of religious groups are disseminating materialistic faith. Some traditional Buddhist groups take that stance, while some

Christian groups in Japan are deeply involved in leftist political activities. A vast number of people have actually begun to lose sight of what the Truth really is.

The cause may lie in the fact that many people do not have spiritual experiences of their own. However, regardless of whether people have actual spiritual experiences or not, they must have had at least one moment during their lives when they instinctively felt a divine power dwelling inside them, a power that comes from a realm they cannot see with their eyes. If they have never felt any such power, that is their own problem.

There are many sacred moments in life: when you realize you are living with the help of many people or are guided by others, when you have managed to rebuild your life with the help of someone's words, or when you feel light guiding you from the invisible world. If you have never experienced such sacred moments in your life, then unfortunately, you cannot say you are successful as a human being.

3

The Mission that Japan, A Major Country, Must Fulfill

✧   ✧   ✧

The theory of evolution is just a hypothesis, not the truth

Japanese people nowadays have an extremely low self-esteem mainly because through school education, they believe that their ancestors were amoebas and that they evolved into humans from simple life forms. I want to ask these people to provide evidence. No one has ever succeeded in proving this.

If there are any living creatures in the process of evolving from amoebas to humans, I want to see them lined up in order, for example, the amoeba forms, the slugs, then snails, etc. If amoebas evolved into humans, the intermediary life forms must have existed and must still exist somewhere. But all the species that exist around us are all complete forms. Only completed species exist now. Think about what this means.

While it is fine to voice opinions based on various hypotheses, they are merely unverified theories, not the truth. You must remember this.

Some people may say that it is too extreme to go as far as claiming that humans are descendants of amoebas. Then, what about a mouse? If nearly a 100 percent of the population believed that humans were descendants of mice, then we could say such a world is insane. Now, a mouse is a mouse and a human is a human, each in completed form.

So, here is my question. If mice remained mice, how did humans become humans? Can anyone explain this? How did humans manage to develop a high level of intelligence and profound emotions, and gain the ability to accomplish intricate work, when mice remained mice? Please explain this. Was it coincidence? Or is this the result of what is known as the survival of the fittest?

To believe that humans came to evolve by chance is the same as saying that trees growing in a forest will naturally turn into wooden houses in time. In reality, however, a house can only be built when there are people who actually cut trees down, turn them into usable lumber, and assemble that lumber into a house.

Calamities on Earth and the creation of New civilizations are two sides of the same coin

Problems are bound to occur in nations that have produced a large number of people who simply accept such completely illogical theories and stop thinking for themselves. We have to fight against the troubles that such nations will face.

It would be nonsense to assume that people who deny their own source of life and reject their dignity would prosper in the future.

Many countries and civilizations in the past have actually perished. On the assumption that the civilization of this island country, Japan, is an independent civilization, as stated by some scholars, the key for this Japanese civilization to continue to flourish even after the 21st century is in the hands of Japanese people. I strongly believe so.

In particular, we absolutely must not allow other nations that are run under mistaken ways of thinking to destroy the Japanese civilization. This will not only stop the Justice of God from being realized on earth, but will produce exactly the opposite outcome. We must consistently assert what is right and continue doing missionary work toward nations that are built upon mistaken national policies from the perspective of the Truth, so that we can turn their current state and culture to head in the right direction. I believe Japan has been allowed to exist as a nation with such great economic power for this purpose. Yet, Japan has not been able to accomplish enough of its mission. This is truly sad.

The Laws of Salvation also states that numerous apocalyptic events will occur from now. It is most likely so; there are already various news reports of flooding and cold waves which are said to be triggered by La Niña [an unusual phenomenon where the sea surface temperature across the equatorial Eastern Central Pacific Ocean drops drastically] and the Arctic oscillation [a phenomenon characterized by the jet stream circulating in different paths depending on the air pressure over the Arctic]. There have been various calamities such as large earthquakes since the turn of this century, and they are likely to continue.

I believe that such shakeup of humanity and the creation of a new civilization are two sides of the same coin. What has existed up to now will be shaken and what has never been imagined will take place. We will see many such incidents in the near future.

I was born to tell of a hopeful future

On December 4, 2010, just before the publication of the book, *The Laws of Salvation*, I gave a grand lecture at Yokohama Arena, located in Kanagawa Prefecture next to Tokyo. In the last five minutes of my lecture, I predicted the coming of the space age, when our exchanges with extraterrestrials will begin [the lecture is included as Chapter One of *Secrets of the Everlasting Truths* (New York: IRH Press, 2012), under the title, "Becoming a World Religion"].

My remarks may have sounded strange to the audience because it was so different from what is commonly accepted in Japan, but when they left the arena, thousands of them witnessed a large formation of UFOs hovering in the sky over Yokohama [see Figure 4]. Many photos were taken of the sighting, and some people even witnessed smaller ships emerge from a mothership. There must have been around 100 UFOs in the skies that day. [The appearance of UFOs was reported in the Japanese sports papers and other publications.]

We have found out that my lectures, broadcast to various locations, are also being tuned into by beings other than the people on Earth. This is unbelievable. Beings from outer space listen to the interpreted lectures of mine, so I need to be more careful about the words I choose. Radio waves are transmitted everywhere, so it must be quite easy for them to pick up and monitor my lectures. Their civilization is high-tech enough to come to Earth, so there is no way they cannot understand my lectures.

I am truly grateful that they take interest in my lectures, but it is a mystery as to what they plan to do with this information. They could use it for good purposes or bad; their true intention is not clear. Nevertheless, I am guessing that they are thoroughly recording which direction Earth's civilization is heading, and whether it is pointing in

Figure 4.
A fleet of UFOs appeared soon after the lecture on December 4, 2010, over the main venue, Yokohama Arena. Many lectures and spiritual readings revealing the truth of people who come to Earth from outer space are recorded and published at Happy Science, one of which is *Breaking the Silence: Interviews with Space People* [Tokyo: Happy Science, 2013].

the same direction that Happy Science is challenging to achieve. In short, I believe they are checking to see whether the people on Earth are able to bring about a brighter future for the planet.

In the summer of 2010, a large mothership was seen hovering over a Chinese airport, which caused havoc, and authorities had no choice but to shut down the airport for a while. The mothership was apparently from the Pleiades star cluster; it gave off an intense light and amazed the people there. Later, we found that it was a warning to China [refer to *Chikyu wo Mamoru "Uchu-rengo" towa Nanika* (literally, "What is the Galactic Federation that Protects the Earth?") (Tokyo: IRH Press, 2011)].

In the near future, phenomena like these that are beyond human control could occur in a variety of ways. Perhaps phenomena we already experienced may happen on a larger scale. Either way, events that are beyond our imagination will most probably occur. At that time, do not lose sight of the right path. I was born to prepare for this time. I have come down to tell you that there is a hopeful future. Please believe this.

4

Eradicating All World Conflicts

✧　　✧　　✧

My true work is that of World Teacher

I have repeatedly said that I am not giving my teachings only for the sake of Japan. While I am serving as National Teacher of Japan, I am essentially World Teacher. My true mission is to indicate to the people of the world, as World Teacher, the direction they should go, or in other words, how our future should be on planet Earth.

For example, in Chapter Four of *The Laws of Salvation* titled, "The Conditions for a Religious Nation," I described from various aspects how the conflict between Islam and Christianity will turn out in the future. The current concern is that the conflict between Israel, which already possesses nuclear weapons, and Iran, where the nuclear weapons are in development and near completion, could escalate into a nuclear war. Another concern is whether Israel would make a preemptive attack against Iran before Iran acquires nuclear capability. If the world approves Iran becoming a nuclear power, then Saudi Arabia and Egypt, too, would no doubt want to arm themselves with nuclear weapons.

Currently in the Middle East, only Israel possesses nuclear weapons while the Islamic nations have none. But what if, in turn,

Israel were to be surrounded by nuclearized Islamic nations? Would the world simply stand back and watch the situation? This is one of the major concerns for the next 10 years or so. If a nuclear war actually breaks out in the Middle East, it would be Armageddon [originally meaning Mount Megiddo], the final battle as predicted in the Old Testament and in the Book of Revelation in the New Testament. This specifically refers to the plains of Megiddo. The concern is whether a final great war will break out in this area.

Differences in religions emerge from The differences in spiritual abilities of their founders

The Laws of Salvation also explains the reasons why those struggles and conflicts take place. In short, humans can only make judgments about God based on what other people say or write because they cannot see the Spirit World through their own eyes. Prophets in the past may have been able to hear the Voice of God, but even they could not see God in most cases. This is a fundamental cause of various conflicts between religions.

For example, we can often find religions that deny idol worship. In many such religions, the founders do not or did not have the ability to see spiritual things. If they were unable to see spiritual things and were only able to hear them or receive spiritual revelations through automatic writing, they would tend to deny idol worship. In contrast, if they were clairvoyant and able to see God and Buddha, they would certainly try to express what they had seen in some kind of visual form.

Usually, those who have actually seen God do not deny idol worship. They will want to show other people exactly how God appears, and will try to make what they saw in the shape of a statue or drawing pictures. In this way, differences in religions arise from the differences in spiritual abilities of the founders.

At the root of world religions is God named "Elohim"

Before I gave the lecture on which this chapter is based, I conducted much spiritual research on the roots of world religions.* I first researched Judaism, a monotheistic religion.

The Lord God in Judaism is called "Yahweh" and, from the outset, Jewish prophets taught people to have faith in Yahweh. There are many such teachings. Moses did the same. However, the name of the Jewish God changed at one point. In the Old Testament, Isaiah, who is regarded as two different people, Proto-Isaiah and Deutero-Isaiah, refers to God as "Elohim." Prior to them, the name of their God was "Yahweh," but from their times it was "Elohim." Jewish people do not know why the name changed; basically, they think the two are the same God.

---

*Refer to *Yahweh, Jehovah, Allah no Shotai wo Tsukitomeru* [literally, "Identifying Yahweh, Jehovah and Allah"] [Tokyo: Happy Science, 2011]

However, the spiritual truth is that the being who Isaiah referred to as "Elohim" was the God that was guiding the region covering the Middle East to Africa at the time. In fact, Elohim became involved around the time of Isaiah to help prepare for Christianity that would be founded by Jesus Christ 700 to 800 years later. Judaism was initially a small religion for the Jewish people in ancient Palestine, but Elohim later became involved in creating the foundation that would allow Christianity, the next world religion, to appear.

Jewish people simply do not understand this. The same was true with Jesus; he was studying the Old Testament and the distinction was not very clear even to him, but still, Jesus believed in Elohim. Elohim was the God of Love who was guiding the entire Middle East at the time. Those who believed in traditional Judaism persecuted Christianity, and later, conflict occurred between Christianity and Islam. As written in *The Laws of Salvation*, the one who guided Islam was also Elohim [Allah], who was in charge of the whole Middle East at that time.

Therefore, the Gods in those three religions are one and the same. However, this has yet to be understood. Furthermore, disputes over the denial of idol worship, as well as the statement, "There is no God besides me," have added to more confusion. Conflicts are now occurring because the different teachings have not been well organized.

The mission of Happy Science is to eradicate All world conflicts and open a bright future

I am now trying to organize and integrate all these teachings. I am trying to clarify what lies at the root of all world religions in order to eradicate all conflicts from the world. I want to correct any misconception or lack of mutual understanding that lie at the root of religious differences before escalation to the use of nuclear weapons. This is how big the mission of Happy Science is.

Happy Science also has a deep understanding of Japanese Shinto, in a way that is completely different from any nationalist right-wing movement. In the past, I have had a great influence on Christianity, Islam, Judaism, and other religions in the world. I have had a major influence on Africa, Egypt, Greece, Rome, and India as well.

And now, I am about to give significant influence to Japan. I have already revealed the Grand Plan for the future and I am determined to make it into reality. The future will not simply be given to us; we must open it with our own efforts. Please hold a strong desire to accomplish it.

Towns with 100 People Who Believe in Me Shall Not See Catastrophic Natural Disasters

I have said before,

"If a town has 100 people who believe in me,

It shall not see catastrophic natural disasters."

An incident to prove my words occurred

In one area in the Tohoku region, northern Japan,

When it was hit by the Great East Japan Earthquake.

I wrote this in *Secrets of the Everlasting Truths*.

In fact, the tsunami avoided the area

Since it had 130 Happy Science believers.

This was often reported in the monthly magazines

And other publications of Happy Science.

Only that very area with 130 believers

Was miraculously spared,

Even though the tsunami brought destruction

To the surrounding areas.

In another case,
The tsunami edged up to a road
Just before the house of an ardent believer,
And then retreated, without reason,
In the opposite direction.

These kinds of miracles happen a lot with Happy Science.
Faith can ultimately work such miracles.

After the Great East Japan Earthquake,
One comment from the media was,
"Faith was powerless in stopping the tsunami,"
Sarcastically referring to Happy Science.

However, the tsunami stopped where it should have
And retreated where it should have.
Those who should have been saved were saved.
Please know this fact.

These miracles are only expedients,
But they are made to occur to teach people
What mystical power is.

Chapter FIVE

What is the Faith in the God of the Earth?

Living in the Age of the New Genesis of Earth

Lecture given on November 2, 2010
at Happy Science General Headquarters, Tokyo, Japan

1

El Cantare is the God of the Earth

✦   ✦   ✦

Happy Science is more than just a Japanese religion

I am currently conducting missionary tours to various overseas countries, and I will also be traveling to countries that are highly risky in terms of my personal security. We are now living in an age of globalization, and traveling has become more convenient than in the past; but should anything happen to me, I would regret it if there were teachings I had failed to give. One topic that I have yet to teach in detail is "El Cantare-belief" so I would like to give the teachings on faith in El Cantare. I am fully prepared to die for the Truth and, considering all the risks, I want to make sure that I have taught all the important teachings. I feel the time has come for me to speak on this topic.

The teachings of Happy Science have become global in scale, and Happy Science is starting to transcend the framework of a Japanese religion. For example, in October 2010, I went to the main island of Okinawa and its neighboring Ishigaki Island in Okinawa Prefecture. The prefecture is located very close to the territorial boundary of Japan and China, and there I spoke about national policies that Japan should adopt. In this way, I believe that Happy Science has begun to transcend the boundaries of religion.

Happy Science is starting to offer information on a far larger scale beyond the sphere of religion, which no other religion today can do. This stance was also apparent when I gave the lecture, "The Resurrection of Religion," at the Aichi Prefectural Gymnasium in October 2010 [the lecture is compiled in Chapter Five of *Kono Kuni wo Mamorinuke* or literally, "Fully Defend This Country," published by the Happiness Realization Party, 2010]. My lecture was broadcast worldwide via satellite, and at that time, I declared my position as World Teacher.

The Happy Science faith has evolved in accordance With the scale of the organization and its teachings

It seems to me that Happy Science faith has undergone several transitions; it evolved and transformed progressively, and is now entering a new stage. In 1986, Happy Science started out in a very small rental office of 10 square meters in Suginami Ward, Tokyo. For about 30 years since that time, the form of our faith has changed and its content has evolved in response to the growing scale of the organization and its teachings.

I began publishing spiritual messages from high spirits starting with Nichiren [refer to *Nichiren no Reigen* (literally, "Spiritual Messages from Nichiren"), currently compiled in *Vols. 1 and 2* of *Ryuho Okawa Collection of Spiritual Messages* (Tokyo: Happy Science)]. In the early days of Happy Science, the spirits in Heaven were considered far superior to the humans living in this world, so we followed their guidance when deciding our activities. However, following the messages of multiple spirits made it difficult to consolidate our faith, as each spirit had a different personality and teaching.

Later, from around 1994, in an effort to simplify our faith, we shifted our focus to the teachings of Buddha* and Hermes†. I stopped publishing spiritual messages and instead published more of my theoretical books. This shift in policy was confusing to our members, producing some who could no longer follow us.

In recent years, I restarted publishing successive spiritual messages. As of November 2017, over 700 spirits have sent us spiritual messages. Some might think that I am simply reverting to our old style, but this is not the case. As I have just mentioned, in the past I used to publish numerous spiritual messages, but a good deal of time has elapsed since then. Accordingly, there are now an increasing number of young people who do not know about the phenomenon of spiritual messages or our past publications of spiritual messages. Moreover, in every era, people want to know about spiritual beings and the Spirit World. Therefore, in order to attract new members and have them take interest in the Spirit World, as well as to help

---

*Buddha, or Gautama Siddhartha, was the founder of Buddhism. Born as a prince of the Shakya clan of India 2,600 years ago, he renounced the world at the age of 29 and later achieved Great Enlightenment. His soul is one of the branch spirits of El Cantare, God of the Earth. Refer to *The Essence of Buddha* [IRH Press, 2016].

† Hermes was a hero and a king of Crete in Greece, who actually existed 4,300 years ago, despite the general belief that he was one of the Olympian gods in the Greek myths. He gave teachings on love and progress, laying the foundation of the current Western civilization. His soul is also a branch spirit of El Cantare, God of the Earth.

them explore their own minds, I have started releasing spiritual messages again.

These spiritual messages serve as a force to spread Happy Science far and wide. In other words, by providing a large variety of teachings that draw people's interest, I am providing many entrance gates to Happy Science. But when such a strong force is at work to expand our movement, it is all the more important to have a strong unifying power, a power that draws people together, to maintain the policy and direction of Happy Science as an organization.

The Happy Science faith Needs to be narrowed down further

I have explained that "El Cantare" is the center or core of the Happy Science faith, and that He has branch spirits named Shakyamuni Buddha, Hermes, Ophealis, Rient Arl Croud, Thoth and Ra Mu [see end section p.188 for more information]. However, in some respects, our faith still has to solidify even further. Although we have already narrowed down the object of faith from a large number of spirits, it is not yet enough. So, now I have come to feel that, in order to establish our faith firmly, we must further organize our thoughts and narrow down our object of faith. This is what we can see past our recent major move, which is beyond the sphere of a mere religion.

I am already thinking far into the future. The organization is following slowly behind me, but it will eventually catch up to my vision.

So I should clearly speak about the direction I am aiming toward.

In the current time being I sometimes refer to myself as the Buddha reincarnated because it is easier for people to understand. However, the time has come for me to explain this faith in more depth. Although some people may recognize the names Gautama Siddhartha and Hermes from history, very few recognize the names of El Cantare's other branch spirits. "El Cantare" is also a name that people have never heard before. Unfamiliarity with the name can become an obstacle to embracing faith in El Cantare.

A concept similar to branch spirits has existed in the past, such as in ancient India. It is said that there were many manifestations of the god Vishnu, one of which was the historical Buddha. The belief in an all-encompassing spirit manifesting itself in offshoots, sending parts of its soul to earth, is quite old and widely accepted knowledge in countries like India. But this notion remains unfamiliar in Christianity and Islam, the monotheistic religions founded within these 2,000 years.

El Cantare-belief acknowledges The existence of the God of the Earth

To be straight, El Cantare-belief is a faith that acknowledges the existence of the God of the Earth. I have been asking you to awaken to this Truth, although it was never explicitly stated. I have yet to teach this straightforwardly, mainly because I am waiting for Happy Science to grow larger and more powerful, from an objective perspective.

A religion can grow larger over time and change its form of faith. For example, Shinran, the founder of the True Pure Land School of Buddhism, proclaimed that he would not accept any disciples but today, the True Pure Land School has become a large organization with an official membership numbering 10 million. The same is true of the Nichiren sect. Although Nichiren referred to himself as just a fellow practitioner of the Lotus Sutra, his organization is now said to have millions of followers. Faith in Shakyamuni Buddha has also changed with the times. Shakyamuni Buddha certainly had human attributes while he was alive, but over time he came to be worshipped as the everlasting Buddha, rather than as a mere human being.

Therefore, it is appropriate to question whether your current image of El Cantare, perceived through the human embodiment called Ryuho Okawa, is the true form of El Cantare. Right now, you are looking at El Cantare in a human form, with human attributes, as if looking through 3-D glasses. El Cantare seen through the eyes of later generations will definitely differ from El Cantare as seen through your eyes now. If you were to ask me which of those images of El Cantare is truer, it would most likely be that of later generations.

The true image of El Cantare Is hard to capture for contemporaries

There are various kinds of delusions, illusions and three-dimensional restrictions in this world that influence people. Therefore, even when a savior is born on earth, people tend to believe in that person as they perceive him or her through their own eyes.

In Christianity, for example, the Jesus seen and believed by his disciples at the time is most probably different from the Jesus that Christians believe in today, 2,000 years later. Jesus' immediate disciples saw him being persecuted and struggling for his next meal or lodgings, just as they were. In the end, Jesus was betrayed by one of his own and, after being stoned by a crowd, was led off by Roman soldiers to be nailed to a cross and executed between two thieves. That was the human image of Jesus Christ. Many of those who witnessed such scenes probably could not believe that he was the savior. In the eyes of later generations, however, the image of Jesus is quite different. Never seeing him in person, Christians today believe in the resurrected Jesus, the only Son of God, and revere him as they would God.

The same was true of Buddhism. The descriptions in the Buddhist scriptures and the detailed precepts during the time of Shakyamuni Buddha give us the impression that he was the kind of person who would give extremely detailed instructions. But the true nature of Shakyamuni Buddha as an object of worship is actually expressed in the great statues of Buddha. In truth, the image held by believers who did not see the historical person is often more accurate.

In the case of Christianity, non-Christians sometimes criticize Jesus saying he could not possibly be the savior, as he could not even save his own life. At the time of his crucifixion, people mocked Jesus. They put a sign on his cross that read "King of the Jews," and placed a crown of thorns on his head instead of an actual crown. They spewed all kinds of verbal abuse and provocations at Jesus, demanding that he save himself if he was indeed the King of the Jews and the savior. Jesus did not actually escape the cross or make something happen to save himself. Through his spiritual resurrection, however, Jesus taught people to believe in the eternal life of the soul. Moreover, by appearing in front of his disciples who were spiritually awakened, Jesus taught people about the true world and the fact that he was an eternal, immortal being.

The Happy Science faith will most likely go through similar transformations as time passes. Unfortunately, in most cases, people living today can only see me to be one-hundredth as great as I really am. Nevertheless, it is interesting to note that, surprisingly, compared to my followers in Japan, those who live in Brazil, a country on the other side of the globe, or in India or the African regions may well hold a truer image of El Cantare in their faith. This happens because human beings tend to perceive things in reference to themselves. Those who can grasp the universal Truth from my teachings in these times while I am alive are highly awakened in the spiritual sense, but in reality, very few can achieve this.

2

The Truth About the Descent
Of El Cantare's Core Consciousness

✧　　✧　　✧

The first descent was under the name
"Alpha" and the second, "Elohim"

I have so far explained that El Cantare has six branch spirits. As for the core part of El Cantare, this is actually the third time that He has descended to earth. His first descent was more than 300 million years ago. At that time, He was called "Alpha." The term "the Laws of Alpha" has sometimes been mentioned in our recordings of various spiritual messages; "Alpha" was His name in His first descent to earth and it means "the beginning" or "origin." So, the laws preached by Alpha are also known as "the Laws of Origin."

The second descent of El Cantare's core consciousness took place around 150 million years ago. His name then was "Elohim," which has generally been shortened to just "El." The name "El" is now known all across the Middle East, Africa and Southern Europe, and is used as a synonym for the word "God." El means "the Light of God," "light" or "God." Thus, "Elohim" was the name of El Cantare's second incarnation.

Alpha decided the direction of Truth for Earth

The core part of El Cantare descended for the first time when a new experiment was being conducted on human civilization on Earth. It was just when the first group of space people immigrated to Earth and new Earthlings were being formed. Since a common set of values for Earth had not yet been developed, the core part descended to earth to teach the Laws under the name "Alpha."

The first group of space people arrived from Zeta, also known as Beta, of the Magellanic Clouds. The word "beta" is still used today, as in "alpha," "beta" and "gamma." A great number of space people came from this planet and lived amongst the humans who had been created on Earth. Around that time, people were in danger of the first conflicts between different races on Earth, or a world war. At the time of such crisis, Alpha was born to integrate the conflicting values and establish a common value system for Earth.

Happy Science has currently been publishing many books of spiritual messages, but if our members do not understand which teachings are true and instead follow whichever teaching or spirit that they fancy at each turn, our organization would be in confusion. The situation of the Earth in Alpha's time was similar to this. If different types of space people tried to instill their own culture from their mother planet on Earth, it would cause confusion. Therefore, it was necessary to define the Truth that was right for Earth and decide the direction of Truth for Earth. That is exactly what was taught in the Laws of Alpha.

As the God of the Earth, Alpha taught Earth's inhabitants to devote themselves to the teachings and made this the condition for them to become Earth people. This was how Alpha unified the human species born on Earth and the immigrants from outer space under the same set of Laws. This is what happened during the first descent of the core part, more than 300 million years ago. There may be an opportunity to give you a more detailed account later on, but for now I just want to teach you that such events occurred [for details, see *The Laws of Alpha* (Tokyo: Happy Science, 2014), and *Alpha no Jidai* (literally, "The Age of Alpha") (Tokyo: IRH Press, 2017)].

Elohim taught the distinction Between light and darkness, good and evil

The core part of El Cantare descended to earth for the second time about 150 million years ago. While Alpha, who taught the Laws of Alpha, was born in the region near present-day Africa, Elohim was born in the western flank of Asia, the region where Europe and Asia meet. This area is very close to the present-day Near and Middle East, the motherland of many religions. Elohim's teachings spread from what is now a desert zone, to Africa, Europe, as well as the region stretching from Caucasus to the east, to the vast Eurasian Continent. The core part descended to earth for the second time to spread His teachings in these regions.

Around that time, the beginning of Hell, or "the lower spirit realm," was forming in the Spirit World. Moreover, various guiding spirits in the heavenly world started to produce different achievements and diverse opinions. This was still before Lucifel* fell to Hell and became Lucifer but among those who had experienced numerous lifetimes on earth, some founded their own religions, whose teachings were much different from the Laws of Alpha, and exerted great influence on people. There were signs that the Earth's Spirit World would eventually develop a large split. Some people were already unable to return to the heavenly world after death, settling themselves in the lower spirit realm. For this reason, people on earth needed to be guided further in the right direction. This is why Elohim was born on earth.

Compared to the Laws of Alpha, what were the main teachings of Elohim? The Laws of Alpha centered on the Genesis or the Laws regarding the creation of humankind. In the time of Elohim, on the other hand, the world was dividing into light and darkness, so Elohim focused on teaching the difference between light and darkness, or good and evil. In other words, He placed emphasis on providing the wisdom to distinguish light and darkness, or good and evil.

Elohim provided much guidance on what was good and what

---

*Lucifel, commonly known as Lucifer, is the devil that rules Hell. He was originally one of the seven archangels, but when he was born on earth about 120 million years ago under the name Satan, he was absorbed by his desires for high-ranking positions and material things, and became corrupt. Being unable to return to Heaven after death, he started his activities to bring confusion in the world. Refer to *The Laws of the Sun* [New York: IRH Press, 2013].

was evil in the context of the Earth. In providing this guidance, He did not neglect to teach that light still exists in what seems evil. Thus, Elohim did not preach a simple dualism of good and evil. He taught that while light can be found in everything, good and evil or light and darkness must be distinguished from the perspective of Truth for Earth, and that humans should always choose light.

These teachings seemingly underlie Zoroastrianism and Manichaeism which came later on. They are somewhat apparent in the teachings of Buddhism as well. As for Christianity, it does not necessarily teach a perfect dualism of good and evil, but since Christianity is a religion that strongly emphasizes the feeling of sin, it can be said that this is also an underlying philosophy of Christianity. This shows that, compared to the first time El Cantare's core part descended to earth, there was a stronger need in the age of His second descent to teach people the difference between good and evil.

The governing principles Elohim taught

At that time, numerous species of space people had already immigrated to Earth. This brought further complexity to the values on Earth. Every star or planet is either advanced or lags behind in different areas, so naturally it is very difficult to try to integrate these differences into a single value system. That being so, Elohim not only taught about good and evil, but also the governing principles that would allow people to rule a country or the world while incorporating different opinions.

The political ideas that laid the foundation of modern democracy are already found in these principles. Elohim taught a concept that was similar to the principle of democracy; people can freely voice their opinions based on different ways of thinking, but if a conclusion is reached after sufficient debate, everyone must follow that ruling. Like modern democracy, Elohim's governing principles also included the ideals of freedom and equality.

El, or Elohim, taught in the following way: "Regardless of whether you were created on Earth or are from outer space, you all have a divine nature or Buddha-nature within and are equally precious as children of God and children of Light. Nevertheless, since everyone has different opinions, you cannot unilaterally unify these opinions. Each individual may speak what he or she believes to be right based on the purity of his or her mind and deep contemplation, but when a decision is reached after thorough discussion, this decision must be implemented and obeyed accordingly.

"Furthermore, if you encounter a problem that cannot be solved by humans, pray to the heavenly world and try to listen to the voice of God. Then, make major decisions based on that voice. You may govern worldly affairs that are left at your discretion by implementing the decisions made through free discussion and majority vote, but when it comes to issues that transcend the human level—issues that go beyond human perception or issues relating to God-created systems that cannot be changed by human decisions—you must follow the Will of God."

Today, Western nations uphold the concepts of freedom and democracy. In the U.S. in particular, the Declaration of Independence, which became the basis of the American Constitution, states that "all men are created equal." Of course, this means that all humans were created equal by God. The principle of freedom works precisely because God created humans as equal.

It is dangerous to give freedom to those who were not created by God, but Elohim taught that because God created all humans, under the principle of equality, they can take action, voice their opinions and carry out various activities in the pursuit of freedom. He taught that, as equal children of God, humans should seek prosperity based on freedom. At the same time, though, Elohim also taught, "Remember that human power is limited and that things beyond human power lie in God's domain. Therefore, you must always remember to devote yourself to the Great Being, when it comes to the mechanism of the universe or the laws governing the universe." These were the main teachings of Elohim.

El Cantare's branch spirits descended to earth And launched new religious movements

Later on, however, different religious sects arose as people chose to adopt various portions of Elohim's teachings. In the Middle East, for example, His teachings were divided and selected in a worldly style, giving birth to many religions based on different parts of the teachings.

In the past, there was even a time when an ethnic god posed as the Supreme God to get the people to believe in him instead. There was also a trend similar to the worship of Baal, where the teaching of prosperity based on freedom was used to arouse worldly desires and lure people away from true faith and spiritual awakening. In fact, the name "Baal" is derived from the word "Belial," which refers to the devil "Beelzebub."

Corruption occurred frequently in various religions in this way. Therefore, the branch spirits of El Cantare were born on earth again and again, and launched new religious movements.

3

Establish Faith in the God of the Earth At the Core of All Religious Beliefs

✧   ✧   ✧

The possibility of crisis for humankind And intervention from outer space

Today, there is a chance of another clash in values or another Cold War on a global scale. In other words, materialistic and atheist countries, which were once thought to have become extinct, are gaining strength and are undergoing revival. Moreover, there is a danger that countries established on a basis of equality, freedom, democracy and prosperity will gradually lose power. Nevertheless, no matter what circumstances may arise, I stand firmly against any regime that rules a nation or the world with materialism, a mistaken belief that denies God. The time is nearer when a world emperor with great military power is very likely to emerge. If a devil were to possess that individual, we may see the birth of a tragic era. So, the time has come to hold the light up high so it will not sink into darkness.

As this great threat approaches humankind, I also predict that another new trend will arise. The next trend we are likely to face is another new intervention from outer space. Right now, discussions are being carried on among space people about topics such as, "Will the civilization on Earth perish?" "Should the current civilization be left as it is?" and "Depending on the situation, it might be necessary to intervene in Earth's civilization at some point in time."

One of the deciding factors for these issues is whether or not an El Cantare civilization based on El Cantare-belief will be successfully established on Earth. If indeed a civilization based on El Cantare-belief prevails on Earth, then beings from outer space will choose to maintain their current attitude as bystanders observing Earth, with as little intervention as possible. However, if the establishment of an El Cantare civilization proves to be merely a mirage or ends as a mere slogan, there may well be new intervention from space. If this were to be the case, the Earth, along with some space people, could be thrown into confusion, and there may come a time when we find ourselves in a similar situation to what happened in the age of Alpha.

Leaving behind "the Laws of the Earth" That people in the future should rely on

Therefore, one of the objectives of my teachings is to clarify the Laws of the Earth that should be handed down to people in the coming Space Age, when humans actually start interacting with beings from outer space. These Laws will probably take full effect after I pass away. All-out interventions will most likely take place once I leave this world. At that time, people will only have my Laws to rely on. I am giving teachings with all of this in mind.

After revealing this much, you probably already understand that my teachings and movement have a much wider perspective and cover a greater range than those of Shakyamuni Buddha, Hermes, Ophealis, Rient Arl Croud, Thoth or Ra Mu. Happy Science is a movement that will determine the major direction that Earth should take. While we must admit the fact that our organization and movement have a long way to go considering the scale of our actual mission, we must not use this as an excuse for our faith not to be rationalized.

Look at the case of Christianity; even his twelve disciples did not stay with Jesus until the end, his crucifixion, but Christianity greatly expanded afterward to cause the Christian civilization to flourish. Although we may not have enough power to influence the entire world right now, I believe our teachings have the power of an immune system that protects the entire planet.

I assume ultimate responsibility for the Earth

The Laws of Alpha explain clearly how and why Earth's spirit group was formed. The Laws of Elohim cover the issues of the dualism of good and evil, which separates Heaven and Hell, and how to dissolve Hell. What I am working on now is to decide how the Earth and the universe should be and how they should interact from now on, while taking into account the Genesis of both the Earth and the universe. At the same time, I have the important role of preventing the further expansion of Hell and strengthening the power of the heavenly world and angels in the Earth sphere.

I called myself "Alpha" in my first incarnation, "Elohim" in my second and now "El Cantare," but the fundamental meaning of these names is the same. They mean "the One," "the Beginning," "the Source," "the Light" and "the Earth." I assume ultimate responsibility for the Earth. This is the foundation upon which "El Cantare-belief" is built.

Therefore, please know that my teachings surpass all the teachings that have been given in the past. Various religions in various countries are allowed to exist under "El Cantare-belief," with the condition that they are working toward preventing the expansion of Hell while expanding the heavenly world. I have absolutely no intention of denying all other religions, but the truth is that this "faith in the God of the Earth" is at the core, from which various other religions and teachings derive.

The true meaning of
"In Heaven and on earth, I alone am to be revered"

Brazil is a country where Catholicism is very strong. India is a country of strong Hinduism, which worships a multitude of gods. Similarly, in the Middle East, another god is being worshipped. But we must teach everyone that there is the Original One. Christians still do not fully understand this point, but if you read the words of Jesus in the Bible, it is clear that he spoke of a Higher Being, the one whom he called "Father," existing on this planet Earth.

In India, during the time of Shakyamuni Buddha, it was believed that Indra was the Supreme God of the Earth. This is similar to Ame-no-Minakanushi-no-Kami [literally, God in the Center of Heaven], revered as the God of the universe in Japanese Shinto. Shakyamuni Buddha, however, clearly states that he was superior to Indra and the various gods supporting Indra. This is one of the reasons the Buddha made the statement, "In Heaven and on earth, I alone am to be revered."

This phrase is sometimes misunderstood, but I must explain its true meaning now: "There is a Being called El Cantare. El Cantare's teachings are the only orthodox Laws, the Laws of Origin. El Cantare-belief is based on a faith in the God of the Earth."

In truth, the teachings of El Cantare did not originate on this Earth. Before He came to Earth, El Cantare was called El Miore and used to rule Venus. El Miore conducted many experiments on civilizations on Venus.

El Cantare invited many space people to Earth, but this does not mean that they were following a completely different god. El Cantare was also involved in the creation of souls of space people on other planets, who have similar ways of thinking as the people on Earth. I believe this fact will be made clear in time. When this fact is revealed, 100 billion years of history will also be revealed.

4

Now is the Beginning of
The New Genesis of Earth

In this chapter, I touched on the topic, "Faith in the God of the Earth" and explained the basic framework of this faith. I do not want people to judge this faith on the basis of today's politics, economics and secular laws, or by the concepts, boundaries and frameworks put forth by various religious beliefs. Try to grasp El Cantare-belief based on the clear understanding that El Cantare is the Origin, Alpha.

My publishing of various spiritual messages, too, is based on this faith. The high spirits of different levels have their own areas of expertise and, under El Cantare-belief, they give opinions based on their own experiences in their respective fields. So, these spiritual messages are not meant to be interpreted as one pleases.

Only when you have faith in El Cantare, will you find the true meaning in those messages.

There are also teachings I gave in my previous incarnations as Buddha and Hermes, as well as the teachings I presented in ancient civilizations as Ra Mu and Thoth which cannot be traced by people today. But El Cantare-belief is not bound even by the earlier teachings given by the branch spirits of El Cantare, either.

The new Genesis of Earth is about to begin right now. Be keenly aware of this.

In the past, I taught that spreading the Laws is the mission of disciples. Indeed, how far and long my disciples spread this faith will determine whether the true form of this faith will be known to later generations. We are still only at the start of a long journey and you still do not know El Cantare in the truest sense. What you are seeing with your eyes is only a part of El Cantare that has manifested as a man living in the same era as you. The image of El Cantare that people will see hundreds and thousands of years later is much closer to the true image of El Cantare. Please understand this.

Chapter SIX

The Choice of Humankind

*Uphold Freedom and Democracy
Under the God of the Earth*

Lecture given on August 2, 2017
at Tokyo Dome, Tokyo, Japan

1

The 21st Century: "Peace and Stability" Or "Shakeout of Humankind"?

✧   ✧   ✧

The significance of my first Tokyo Dome lecture in 22 years

This chapter is based on the lecture I gave in Tokyo Dome on August 2, 2017 [see Figure 5]. By the end of 1995, I had already given 10 lectures at Tokyo Dome. Those who were not yet born back then have now become Happy Science staff and active members. I am very happy about this. Since that time, we have been moderately but steadily carrying out various activities and spreading the teachings throughout Japan and the world. I have published over 2,300 books and have given over 2,600 lectures [as of November 2017]. The number of people who have heard my lectures has now reached over several hundred million.

On the night of August 2, the lecture was broadcast live to about 3,500 locations around the world, but it could not be heard right away in some countries. Some people had to wait until October to listen to my lecture. This makes me feel how vast the world is.

It takes a boundlessly deep and heavy responsibility to provide teachings to the entire world. But I have been doing this for more than 30 years now. When I gave my first Tokyo Dome lecture in 1991, the name Happy Science became widely known throughout the country, but our event must have appeared like a strange gathering of a new religious group. I am afraid some of our members faced various troubles because people in general did not yet have a clear understanding of Happy Science.

Since then, we have spread our teachings throughout the world, and now I have gained some confidence. Is there anyone else on Earth who can give teachings to the world from Tokyo Dome? This is the meaning of my being here and teaching you the Truth. Please let the

Figure 5.
A photo of the main venue of the special lecture, "The Choice of Humankind" given on August 2, 2017 at Tokyo Dome.

future generations know that the Lord did not forsake humankind in the early 21st century.

The world's population has now exceeded seven billion and it is quite challenging to bring the teachings to all people. However, whether the 21st century will be a century of peace and stability or whether a shakeout will occur for the overpopulated humankind depends on the actions of you, who live today, and those who will follow in your footsteps.

Why did I give a lecture in Tokyo Dome for the first time in 22 years? It is because now is the time that will determine the future of humankind, and now is the very moment when we have reached the summit of a mountain.

Alpha: the God of Origin and the God of Creation

It was 300 or 400 million years ago when I aspired to create humankind. Although modern science does not admit this, human ancestors were first born on earth more than 300 million years ago when dinosaurs still roamed the planet.

In the initial stage, I allowed three kinds of people to live on earth. There were already spiritual beings existing in the Earth's sphere, so I first sent several hundred of them to manifest in a physical form on earth. There were also different space people who had come from other stars, so I also chose those who could adapt to the Earth's environment and sent them to earth. Another type from outer space not fit for the Earth's environment needed to change their physical bodies for life suited on Earth; I allowed them to be hybrids before I sent them on to earth. These were the three kinds of humans to live on earth in the founding period of humankind.

Around that time, I was born on earth with the name "Alpha." It is the name of the first leader of humankind. This is the very beginning of how "El Cantare" came to be called "the Lord."

The name was Alpha, "the God of Origin" and "the God of Creation."

Humankind witnessed the rise and fall of Seven civilizations in these one million years

Since first descending to earth, I have tried various things in an effort to create something new. I also formed many civilizations in order to reconcile and harmonize people with different ways of thinking and characteristics, and make them one as people of Earth. However, many among them could not understand my ideas; they engaged in war due to differences in race or skin color. Even so, I have been watching over the gradual evolution and progress of humankind with a heart of tolerance for 330 million years.

There still exist racism and racial discrimination due to skin color, even today. Also, there are different levels of economic development and intelligence between countries. How each country values human life is different, too; the value of a person's life in one country might be one percent of that of someone in another country.

I have made many different attempts over a long period of time. I have sent in various saviors to this world, sometimes in the same era. Then, ethnic religions were founded around those saviors. However, ethnic religions that were originally founded by the Love of God eventually led people to mutually distrust and doubt each other, giving rise to battles where different groups tried to ostracize each other. This happened countless times in the past.

I will not give you the long story here because you probably do not need to hear what spans hundreds of millions of years. But I can at least say that humankind has experienced and witnessed the rise and fall of seven civilizations in the last one million years or so. In this meaning, "civilization" implies one in the large sense, as to whether a whole continent prospers or disappears. The one flourishing now is the seventh civilization. Whether this seventh civilization will perish or continue onward depends on the present. (*The Laws of the Sun* [New York: IRH Press, 2013] states that there were the Garna, Myutram, Lamudia, Mu and Atlantis Civilizations in the past one million years. In addition, there was the Asgard Civilization which mainly prospered in Northern Europe and interacted with space beings, between the Atlantis Civilization and the current one. It is the root of pre-Christian religions in Europe. The Asgard Civilization was started by Odin, Thor and Loki, and had much influence on the Egyptian and Greek Civilizations, but declined due to drop in agricultural production caused by climate cooling.)

2

Various Nuclear Crises the World is Facing

✦   ✦   ✦

North Korea's nuclear development is now inviting
A critical moment for the third time

I would assume you know one of the greatest problems in current world affairs. A "fire" is about to be lit in Asia—the nuclear development and the ballistic missile tests by North Korea. North Korea is aiming to equip themselves, so that they can fight on equal terms with the U.S. Of course, from their point of view, they are strengthening their military power to defend themselves and to protect their country from possible U.S. attacks. But what do their actions look like from the U.S. point of view?

North Korea already possesses Intercontinental Ballistic Missiles [ICBMs] that can reach the mainland U.S., and they have even succeeded in atomic bomb and hydrogen bomb tests. There is no way that the U.S. will remain silent and allow North Korea to continue as it is. Some people believe there is still room for negotiations while others say the time for talks is over. In the lecture on August 2, I stated that the U.S. would at most come to a conclusion within a month. Whatever their decision, it would determine the future of humankind.*

This is the third time that the U.S. is struggling over North Korea's nuclear threat. The first time was in 1994, when North Korea was suspected of nuclear development during the Clinton administration. At that time, the Clinton administration seriously considered an attack on North Korea's nuclear facilities. But a computer simulation predicted that at least a million South Koreans and a hundred thousand Americans would die. On seeing the simulation results, then-South Korean President Kim Young-sam, who is considered the political mentor of the current President Moon Jae-in, demanded that the U.S. refrain from attacking North Korea, saying that he could not afford to let a million people die. Having failed to gain the consent of South Korea, the U.S. called off the attack and held talks instead. As a result, the first leader of North Korea, Kim Il-sung, agreed to freeze their nuclear weapons development project.

Around that time, I gave a public lecture and pointed out the dangers of North Korea's nuclear development, stating the need for a countermeasure [the lecture was later published as *Utopia Sozo-ron* (literally, "On the Creation of Utopia") (Tokyo: IRH Press, 1997)]. I also gave a warning through *The Terrifying Revelations*

---

* Later, in *Donald Trump vs. Kim Jong-un: A Spiritual Battle between Two Leaders* [Tokyo: HS Press, 2017] [spiritual interview recorded on Aug. 29], the guardian spirit of Donald Trump spoke his true thoughts: "We will destroy all the country [of North Korea]." On Sept. 19, Donald Trump himself gave a speech at the UN General Assembly, giving a strong warning similar to his guardian spirit: "...if it [America] is forced to defend itself or its allies, we will have no choice but to totally destroy North Korea."

of Nostradamus [executive producer Ryuho Okawa], the very first movie by Happy Science, which was released in theaters throughout Japan in 1994. It depicted the North Korean nuclear missile crisis. I had already been giving warnings about North Korea from that time.

The second crisis was from 2008 to 2009, when Kim Jong-il was the leader of North Korea. At that time, North Korea decided to push further with their nuclear development. Unfortunately, the U.S. had changed from a Republican to a Democratic administration led by Obama. At the same time, a great global recession was triggered by the bankruptcy of Lehman Brothers. These events kept the U.S. from taking action against North Korea's nuclear development. The U.S. missed these two chances to shut down North Korea.

Now, with the third leader Kim Jong-un in power, North Korea is trying to finish the job. This is what Kim Jong-un is aiming to do during his regime. It is unfortunate, indeed.

As for myself, I am working quickly to prepare to accept the souls of over a million people in the Spirit World in case a war breaks out. In the near future, the decision of the U.S. will become apparent to the world. If the U.S. takes action, North Korea will collapse at the expense of a great number of lives. On the other hand, if the U.S. does not take action, that is to say, if President Trump lacks decision-making ability, the U.S. will most probably lose its superpower status and will no longer reign as the world hegemon. We will no longer see any country listening to what the U.S. has to say.

The nuclear situation in Asia and the Middle East

Crises are already everywhere in the world. For example, there is friction between China and India. Nearby are Bhutan and Nepal. These countries are fearful of an invasion by China. India is now quite irritated, and there could be a nuclear war with China at any moment. In such times, a crisis cannot be ended unless there is a leader in the world.

There were several such crises in the past. Another example was the Cuban Missile Crisis in 1962. The Soviets built a missile base on the island of Cuba. If Cuba had been equipped with nuclear arms, the entire U.S. would have fallen within the range of nuclear missiles. Then-President Kennedy established a naval quarantine around the island, commonly known as the naval blockade, and demanded that Russia withdraw from Cuba. Soviet Premier Khrushchev finally agreed. In this way, the crisis of a nuclear war was averted.

There have been other nuclear crises besides these. India and Pakistan were once on the verge of nuclear war.* Israel is constantly posing a nuclear threat to the surrounding Arab nations because Israel believes they need nuclear weapons to protect their small country. In response, Iran will probably be the next country to pose the problem of nuclear development after North Korea.

---

*India and Pakistan both declared independence in 1947. They have been in conflict and have fought three wars over Kashmir. In 1974, India conducted underground nuclear tests, declaring itself to be a nuclear power. In 1998, both India and Pakistan conducted underground nuclear tests successively, raising the tensions of a nuclear crisis between the two countries.

3

The Status Quo of Various Countries In Light of World Justice

National defense based on patriotism is essential to stabilize and develop a country. I agree that this is true. Just as a local region is allowed to govern itself in a country, it is a matter of course that nearly 200 countries on Earth each work on national security to defend themselves. However, this is just one yardstick, and is not the only one. There needs to be another measure that asks whether a country's actions to defend itself are in accordance with world justice. This is the important point.

There are extremely difficult issues in the world today. For example, currently, the leader of North Korea does not listen to the voices of the world at all. The Chinese president hardly recognizes the difference between domestic and international laws. Russia is a nation that is half dictatorship, but the other half is seeking freedom and democracy, aiming to officially resurrect the Russian Orthodox Church. To consider these problems, let me illustrate the differences among countries in the following example:

The U.S.

In the U.S., when Donald Trump stepped forward as a presidential candidate, the mass media harshly criticized him during his election campaign. Criticisms against him continue now, even after he became president. Taking the lead in those criticisms has been CNN, a major international TV station. One of their main newscasters seems to be very hostile to President Trump, and is strongly opposed to him. However, I am sure that the newscaster does not fear for his life. This is the U.S.

Russia

What would happen if the main newscaster from a major broadcaster in Russia continued to criticize President Putin? He would certainly be assassinated. Something similar actually happened in the past.

China

What would happen if a big TV station in China pointed out the wrongdoings of the Chinese government or Xi Jinping? The newscaster of that station would of course be sent to prison. The least that might happen to the newscaster would be to end up like Mr. Liu Xiaobo,* but he or she would most likely be purged. The station would dissolve by being nationalized. In fact, Xi Jinping himself has been the target of assassination more than six times in the past.

---

* Liu Xiaobo [1955 – 2017] was a Chinese human rights activist. In 1989, he was imprisoned after conducting a hunger strike during the Tiananmen Square incident. In 2008, he drafted and announced "Charter 08." Due to this, he was sentenced to 11 years in prison in 2010. In the same year, he received a Nobel Peace Prize while in jail. In 2017, he was diagnosed with terminal liver cancer, and passed away in a hospital outside the prison [refer to *Spiritual Interview with Liu Xiaobo: The Fight for Freedom Continues* (Tokyo: HS Press, 2017)].

Among the successive leaders in China, he is known as the one who fears assassination the most. This is certainly why he tries to continuously put on a show of aggressive leadership. This is China.

North Korea

What about North Korea? There would be no CNN-like media in the first place. If you look at the people of North Korea in the various news media, the only one truly smiling is Kim Jong-un. It is a completely totalitarian nation, or one of socialist totalitarianism. China is similar to North Korea, but China is a little lenient because there is still some competition for power. It would take some time to change this.

Japan

What would happen if such an organization like CNN continued to criticize Prime Minister Abe? Prime Minister Abe would probably invite the head of that media to have dinner together to try persuasion. He may even take him or her golfing. If the criticisms do not stop there, then Mr. Abe might have one of his cabinet members resign, but eventually he, himself, would end up resigning. This is Japan.

All countries have different circumstances and each would respond in a different way. Please consider carefully which country you would choose to be born into if you were to start your life afresh. Justice of God lies in the country you would want to be born into, even after knowing each country's circumstances. It is a painful choice to make, but you cannot escape God's eyes to decide whether or not the country you want to defend deserves to be defended. I clearly state this.

While people in all countries have the right to love and defend their country, there is another measure that asks whether that country which people want to defend is righteous from the perspective of world justice, or the Will of God. We must not forget this perspective.

4

Humankind Now Stands
At an Important Crossroads

✧　　✧　　✧

The problem of separation of Religion and state in free and democratic nations

On one hand, there are the socialist totalitarian nations, or the totalitarian nations in which politics and economy only move in accordance with the rules determined by their government. In such nations, freedom of speech, freedom of expression, and freedom of the press including publications and media are significantly restricted. On the other hand, there are the free and democratic nations where all those freedoms are allowed. They may still have many problems to solve, but they are seeking justice in their own nations.

To put it differently, it comes down to two choices. One is that the national framework of freedom and democracy based on the U.S. and Japan continues to lead the world from 2017 onward. The other is that we accept totalitarian nations like North Korea and China, which have no freedom of the press or freedom of speech, to rule the world through fear. We are now being asked to choose between these two. The year 2017 was one of the vital years to decide this. The important issues have now narrowed down to this.

We need to brace ourselves against what is to come. We need to be courageous. There will be many opinions that may well confuse people. There will be many opposing views. The race to move international opinion will heat up. But if you get confused, then in the end, listen to my words. They are the words of the One who has been guiding humankind.

I am hoping that essentially, nations will be run in a way to fulfill the Words of God. However, there is no such nation in the world today. Nations of freedom and democracy are certainly far better than nations that suppress individual human rights and easily kill their people. But people in many of these countries are unable to feel the Words of God; they consider His teachings to be things of the past. Please know this.

The key phrase is, "separation of religion and state." Many free and democratic nations separate politics from religion. This is why Christian countries can wage war against each other even though Jesus taught, "You shall not kill." In other words, since they separate church and state, their politics are managed by the elected delegates, not by God. That is why they can kill. This is the issue regarding separation of religion and state.

The problem of monotheism in theocratic countries

On the other hand, there are nations where religion and politics are united. These countries try to reflect God's teachings in their political and economic institutions. Islamic countries are one example. If the true Will of God were genuinely reflected in their politics, they should produce the right outcome.

Unfortunately, however, it has been 1,400 years since Muhammad's descent and the leaders of Islamic nations cannot understand the mind of Muhammad straightforwardly. For this reason, while they do refer to past scriptures, they adopt political and economic policies that only serve to their advantage today. Even theocracy, the unity of religion and state, has such problems.

Historically, many Islamic countries are strongly connected to monarchism, so they tend to dislike democracy. That is why some people who immigrate to Western countries from Islamic countries become terrorists and cause disturbances in the world. While some Muslim believers agree with democracy, the so-called radicals or fundamentalists do not approve of democracy because they believe that humans should live as God has ordered.

The problem is that the current leaders of Islam are unable to hear the Words of God. If they could hear His Words, they could reflect on themselves and change their ways of thinking. Those who were able to hear the Words of God were the people in the very old, classical age. Although Islamic leaders today try to make decisions on current politics or economy based on the words from ancient times, they cannot because those words do not mention anything about current affairs.

There are suicide bombings by Muslims, when in fact Allah teaches that murder is wrong in the Koran. It teaches not to kill or hurt others. Despite this, they go to war because they believe that their God is the true God and all other gods are false. But they need to know that monotheism is not the one and only way of religion.

Historically speaking, every race or country has its own so-called "God." I acknowledge this. Thus, polytheism as practiced in India is indeed true; there are a countless number of gods. If people believed theirs was the only one true God and all others were fake, wars would break out all the time because attacking and occupying other countries in an effort to spread their teachings to other ethnicities would be justified.

Christianity is another monotheistic religion, which helps explain why Spain and Portugal in earlier times traveled across the world and colonized many countries. They destroyed religions in various countries and colonized them. Despite that, Christianity is still unable to govern the entire world. This is not God's fault. The problem lies in the level of awareness of those who believe in and practice the teachings of God.

5

Message from El Cantare, God of the Earth

Now, I tell you this.
"Lord God" in Christianity,
"Elohim" in Judaism,
"Allah" in Islam,
"Shangdi," or the emperor in Heaven,
Referred to by Confucius of China,
And "Ame-no-Mioya-Gami" in Japanese Shinto,
The one above the central god Ame-no-Minakanushi-no-Kami
And whose profile remains unknown,
Are all the same, single Being.

Religions differ in their ways of thinking
Due to differences in racial characteristics and cultural traits.
However, there is only one origin;
People are all friends undergoing soul training together on earth
As they refine their souls in various ways.

I created the system of reincarnation,
So that people can go beyond the barrier between ethnic groups.

Although you may be Japanese today,

You may have been European, Chinese, Korean, or another

In your past lives, or vice versa.

By going through such soul experiences,

Perhaps experiencing past lives as both male and female,

You are trying to broaden your capacity to understand each other.

I was born in this land of Japan

In order to teach the last, the final, and all Laws.

I will reveal everything I know.

From now on,

You must not start an international war because of religion.

You must not start a war

Because of conflicts between atheism and theism,

Or whether one has faith or not.

Kim Jong-un, believe in God!

Abandon nuclear weapons!

Abandon missiles!

Xi Jinping, acknowledge God!

Acknowledge freedom and democracy under God!

These are the Words of the God of the Earth.

I also tell Islamic nations.

You profess monotheism, but can you hear the Voice of God?

If you want to hear it, listen to my words.
Then, Muslims and Europeans shall no longer fight
By using terrorist attacks over immigration issues.
I do not encourage such a thing.
I do not approve of civilians attacking other civilians
By driving a car bomb into them.
I do not approve of mothers or children,
Wrapped in dynamite,
Committing suicidal terrorism in crowds of people,
Instilling fear into tens of thousands.

I say unto you.
Humankind must learn the Words of the True God,
Overcome their differences, reconcile and harmonize,
And strive to evolve and develop.
These are the Words of El Cantare, God of the Earth.
You shall not forget this ever again.
Engrave this into your heart.

Humankind is one.
From now on,
Believe in the existence of the God who surpasses worldly conflicts
And, under God,
Choose to continue with the world
That upholds freedom and democracy.

I will say it again.

What North Korea needs is faith.

What China needs is faith, too.

What India needs is the God above various gods.

What the Islamic nations need is to learn who Allah is.

I love and accept humankind beyond their differences.

Through believing,

Learn what love is.

This is my message.

AFTERWORD

I declare to people in Japan and the world today who are overwhelmed by the torrent of trivial information.

This book is the modern Bible and Koran.

It describes the core teachings of a global-scale world religion that comes after Christianity and Islam.

Eventually, you will have to call the name of God.

To teach the name of God is the mission of this book.

To believe is also to love yourself, a soul with eternal life.

Ryuho Okawa
Founder and CEO of Happy Science Group
December 2017

*This book is a compilation of the lectures,
with additions, as listed below.*

- Chapter One -
The Power to Believe

Japanese title: *Shinjiru Chikara*
Lecture given on February 11, 2017
at Beppu International Convention Center, B-Con Plaza, Oita, Japan

- Chapter Two -
Starting from Love

Japanese title: *Ai kara Hajimaru*
Lecture given on July 9, 2017
at Tokyo Shoshinkan, Tokyo, Japan

- Chapter Three -
The Gate to the Future

Japanese title: *Mirai eno Tobira*
Lecture given on January 9, 2017
at Pacifico Yokohama, Kanagawa, Japan

- Chapter Four -
The World Religion of Japanese Origin Will Save the Earth

Japanese title: *Nihon Hatsu Sekai Shukyo ga Chikyu wo Sukuu*

Lecture title: *Kyusei no Ho Kogi*

Lecture given on January 16, 2011

at Tokyo Shoshinkan, Tokyo, Japan

- Chapter Five -
What is the Faith in the God of the Earth?

Japanese title: *Chikyushin eno Shinko towa nanika*

Lecture title: *El Cantare Shinko towa nanika*

Lecture given on November 2, 2010

at Happy Science General Headquarters, Tokyo, Japan

- Chapter Six -
The Choice of Humankind

Japanese title: *Jinrui no Sentaku*

Lecture given on August 2, 2017

at Tokyo Dome, Tokyo, Japan

* *Life-Changing Words* are quoted from other books by the author.

WHAT IS EL CANTARE?

El Cantare means "the Light of the Earth," and is the Supreme God of the Earth who has been guiding humankind since the beginning of Genesis. He is whom Jesus called Father, and His branch spirits, such as Buddha and Hermes, have descended to Earth many times and helped to flourish many civilizations. To unite various religions and to integrate various fields of study in order to build a new civilization on Earth, a part of the core consciousness has descended to Earth as Master Ryuho Okawa.

El Cantare,
God of the Earth

Ra Mu

Gautama
Siddhartha

Thoth

Hermes

Rient Arl Croud   Ophealis

Ryuho Okawa

Buddha

Gautama Siddhartha was born as a prince into the Shakya Clan in India around 2,600 years ago. When he was 29 years old, he renounced the world and sought enlightenment. He later attained Great Enlightenment and founded Buddhism.

Hermes

In the Greek mythology, Hermes is thought of as one of the 12 Olympian gods, but the spiritual Truth is that he taught the teachings of love and progress around 4,300 years ago that became the origin of the rise of the Western civilization. He is a hero that truly existed.

Ophealis

Ophealis was born in Greece around 6,500 years ago and was the leader who took an expedition to as far as Egypt. He is the God of miracles, prosperity, and arts, and is known as Osiris in the Egyptian mythology.

Rient Arl Croud

Rient Arl Croud was born as a king of the ancient Incan Empire around 7,000 years ago and taught about the mysteries of the mind. In the heavenly world, he is responsible for the interactions that take place between various planets.

Thoth

Thoth was an almighty leader who built the golden age of the Atlantic civilization around 12,000 years ago. In the Egyptian mythology, he is known as god Thoth.

Ra Mu

Ra Mu was a leader who built the golden age of the civilization of Mu around 17,000 years ago. As a religious leader and a politician, he ruled by uniting religion and politics.

WHAT IS A SPIRITUAL MESSAGE?

We are all spiritual beings living on this earth. The following is the mechanism behind Ryuho Okawa's spiritual messages.

1 You are a spirit

People are born into this world to gain wisdom through various experiences and return to the other world when their lives end. We are all spirits and repeat this cycle in order to refine our souls.

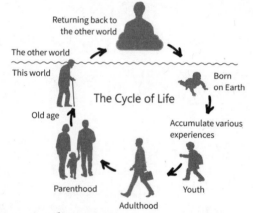

2 You have a guardian spirit

Guardian spirits are those who protect the people living on this earth. Each of us has a guardian spirit that watches over us and guides us from the other world. They are one of our past lives, and are identical in how we think.

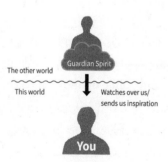

3 How spiritual messages work

Since a guardian spirit thinks at the same subconscious level as the person living on earth, Ryuho Okawa can summon the spirit and find out what the person on earth is actually thinking. If the person has already returned to the other world, the spirit can give messages to the people living on earth through Ryuho Okawa.

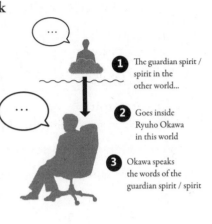

1 The guardian spirit / spirit in the other world...

2 Goes inside Ryuho Okawa in this world

3 Okawa speaks the words of the guardian spirit / spirit

The spiritual messages of more than 700 sessions have been openly recorded by Ryuho Okawa since 2009, and the majority of these have been published. Spiritual messages from the guardian spirits of living politicians such as U.S. President Trump, Japanese Prime Minister Shinzo Abe and Chinese President Xi Jinping, as well as spiritual messages sent from the Spirit World by Jesus Christ, Muhammad, Thomas Edison, Mother Teresa, Steve Jobs and Nelson Mandela are just a tiny pack of spiritual messages that were published so far.

Domestically, in Japan, these spiritual messages are being read by a wide range of politicians and mass media, and the high-level contents of these books are delivering an impact even more on politics, news and public opinion. In recent years, there have been spiritual messages recorded in English, and English translations are being done on the spiritual messages given in Japanese. These have been published overseas, one after another, and have started to shake the world.

For more about spiritual messages and a complete list of books, visit okawabooks.com

ABOUT HAPPY SCIENCE

Happy Science is a global movement that empowers individuals to find purpose of life and spiritual happiness and to share that happiness with their families, societies, and the world. With more than 12 million members around the world, Happy Science aims to increase awareness of spiritual truths and expand our capacity for love, compassion, and joy so that together we can create the kind of world we all wish to live in. Teachings of Happy Science are based on the Exploration of the Right Mind and the Principles of Happiness (Love, Wisdom, Self-Reflection, and Progress).

Love teaches us to give ourselves freely without expecting anything in return; it encompasses giving, nurturing, and forgiving.

Wisdom leads us to the insights of spiritual truths, and opens us to the true meaning of life and the will of God (the universe, the highest power, Buddha).

Self-Reflection brings a mindful, nonjudgmental lens to our thoughts and actions to help us find our truest selves—the essence of our souls—and deepen our connection to the highest power. It helps us attain a clean and peaceful mind and leads us to the right life path.

Progress emphasizes the positive, dynamic aspects of our spiritual growth—actions we can take to manifest and spread happiness around the world. It's a path that not only expands our soul growth, but also furthers the collective potential of the world we live in.

These teachings embrace worldwide philosophies and beliefs, transcending boundaries of culture and religions.

Programs and Events

The doors of Happy Science are open to all. We offer a variety of programs and events, including self-exploration and self-growth programs, spiritual seminars, meditation and contemplation sessions, study groups, and book events.

Our programs are designed to:

- Deepen your understanding of your purpose and meaning in life
- Improve your relationships and increase your capacity to love unconditionally
- Attain a peace of mind, decrease anxiety and stress, and feel positive
- Gain deeper insights and broader perspective on the world
- Learn how to overcome life's challenges
  . . . and much more.

For more information, visit happyscience-na.org or happy-science.org.

International Seminars

Each year, friends from all over the world join our international seminars, held at our faith centers in Japan. Different programs are offered each year and cover a wide variety of topics, including improving relationships, practicing the Eightfold Path to enlightenment, and loving yourself, to name just a few.

Happy Science Monthly

Our monthly publication covers the latest featured lectures, members' life-changing experiences and other news from members around the world, book reviews, and many other topics. Downloadable PDF files are available at happyscience-na.org. Copies and back issues in Portuguese, Chinese, and other languages are available upon request. For more information, contact us via e-mail at <u>tokyo@happy-science.org</u>.

CONTACT INFORMATION

Happy Science is a worldwide organization with faith centers around the globe. For a comprehensive list of centers, visit the worldwide directory at happy-science.org or happyscience-na.org. The following are some of the many Happy Science locations:

UNITED STATES AND CANADA

New York
79 Franklin Street
New York, NY 10013
Phone: 1-212-343-7972
Fax: 1-212-343-7973
Email: ny@happy-science.org
Website: newyork.happyscience-na.org

New Jersey
725 River Rd. #102B
Edgewater, NJ 07020
Phone: 1-201-313-0127
Fax: 1-201-313-0120
Email: nj@happy-science.org
Website: newjersey.happyscience-na.org

San Francisco
525 Clinton Street
Redwood City, CA 94062
Phone & Fax: 1-650-363-2777
Email: sf@happy-science.org
Website: sanfrancisco.happy
science-na.org

Atlanta
1874 Piedmont Ave.
NE Suite 360-C
Atlanta, GA 30324
Phone: 1-404-892-7770
Email: atlanta@happy-science.org
Website: atlanta.happyscience-na.org

Florida
5208 8th St. Zephyrhills, FL 33542
Phone: 1-813-715-0000
Fax: 1-813-715-0010
Email: florida@happy-science.org
Website: florida.happyscience-na.org

Los Angeles
1590 E. Del Mar Blvd.
Pasadena, CA 91106
Phone: 1-626-395-7775
Fax: 1-626-395-7776
Email: la@happy-science.org
Website: losangeles.happyscience-na.org

Orange County
10231 Slater Ave #204
Fountain Valley, CA 92708
Phone: 1-714-745-1140
Email: oc@happy-science.org

San Diego
7841 Balboa Ave
Suite #202
San Diego, CA 92111
Phone: 1-619-381-7615
Fax: 1-626-395-7776
Email: sandiego@happy-science.org
Website: happyscience-la.org

Hawaii

Email: hi@happy-science.org
Website: hawaii.happyscience-na.org

Kauai

4504 Kukui Street
Dragon Building Suite 21
Kapaa, HI 96746
Phone: 1-808-822-7007
Fax: 1-808-822-6007
Email: kauai-hi@happy-science.org
Website: kauai.happyscience-na.org

Toronto
845 The Queensway, Etobicoke,
ON, M8Z 1N6 Canada
Phone: 1-416-901-3747
Email: toronto@happy-science.org
Website: happy-science.ca

Vancouver
#212-2609 East 49th Avenue, Vancouver,
BC,V5S 1J9 Canada
Phone: 1-604-437-7735
Fax: 1-604-437-7764
Email: vancouver@happy-science.org
Website: happy-science.ca

INTERNATIONAL

Tokyo
1-6-7 Togoshi, Shinagawa
Tokyo, 142-0041 Japan
Phone: 81-3-6384-5770
Fax: 81-3-6384-5776
Email: tokyo@happy-science.org
Website: happy-science.org

London
3 Margaret Street
London, W1W 8RE
United Kingdom
Phone: 44-20-7323-9255
Fax: 44-20-7323-9344
Email: eu@happy-science.org
Website: happyscience-uk.org

Sydney

516 Pacific Hwy Lane Cove North,
NSW 2066 Australia
Phone: 61-2-9411-2877
Fax: 61-2-9411-2822
Email: sydney@happy-science.org

Brazil Headquarters

Rua. Domingos de Morais 1154,
Vila Mariana, Sao Paulo,
SP-CEP 04009-002 Brazil
Phone: 55-11-5088-3800
Fax: 55-11-5088-3806
Email: sp@happy-science.org
Website: happyscience.com.br

Jundiai

Rua Congo, 447, Jd. Bonfiglioli
Jundiai, SP-CEP 13207-340 Brazil
Phone: 55-11-4587-5952
Email: jundiai@happy-sciece.org

Seoul

74, Sadang-ro 27-gil,
Dongjak-gu, Seoul, Korea
Phone: 82-2-3478-8777
Fax: 82-2- 3478-9777
Email: korea@happy-science.org
Website: happyscience-korea.org

Taipei

No. 89, Lane 155, Dunhua N. Road
Songshan District, Taipei City 105, Taiwan
Phone: 886-2-2719-9377
Fax: 886-2-2719-5570
Email: taiwan@happy-science.org
Website: happyscience-tw.org

Malaysia

No 22A, Block2, Jalil Link, Jalan
Jalil Jaya 2, Bukit Jalil 57000
Kuala Lumpur, Malaysia
Phone: 60-3-8998-7877
Fax: 60-3-8998-7977
Email: Malaysia@happy-science.org
Website: happyscience.org.my

Nepal

Kathmandu Metropolitan City
Ward No. 15, Ring Road,
Kimdol, Sitapaila,
Kathmandu, Nepal
Phone: 977-1-427-2931
Email: nepal@happy-science.org

Uganda

Plot 877 Rubaga Road,
Kampala P.O. Box 34130
Kampala, Uganda
Phone: 256-79-3238-002
Email: uganda@happy-science.org
Website: happyscience-uganda.org

HAPPINESS REALIZATION PARTY

The Happiness Realization Party (HRP) was founded in May 2009 by Master Ryuho Okawa as part of the Happy Science Group to offer concrete and proactive solutions to the current issues such as military threats from North Korea and China and the long-term economic recession. HRP aims to implement drastic reforms of the Japanese government, thereby bringing peace and prosperity to Japan. To accomplish this, HRP proposes two key policies:

1) Strengthening the national security and the Japan-US alliance which plays a vital role in the stability of Asia.

2) Improving the Japanese economy by implementing drastic tax cuts, taking monetary easing measures and creating new major industries.

HRP advocates that Japan should offer a model of a religious nation that allows diverse values and beliefs to coexist, and that contributes to global peace.

*For more information, visit **en.hr-party.jp***

HAPPY SCIENCE UNIVERSITY

★ This is an unaccredited institution of higher education.

The Founding Spirit and the Goal of Education

Based on the founding philosophy of the university, "Pursuit of happiness and the creation of a new civilization," education, research and studies will be provided to help students acquire deep understanding grounded in religious belief and advanced expertise with the objectives of producing "great talents of virtue" who can contribute in a broad-ranging way to serve Japan and the international society.

Faculties

Faculty of Human Happiness

Students in this faculty will pursue liberal arts from various perspectives with a multidisciplinary approach, explore and envision an ideal state of human beings and society.

Faculty of Successful Management

This faculty aims to realize successful management that helps organizations to create value and wealth for society and to contribute to the happiness and the development of management and employees as well as society as a whole.

Faculty of Future Creation

Students in this faculty study subjects such as political science, journalism, performing arts and artistic expression, and explore and present new political and cultural models based on truth, goodness and beauty.

Faculty of Future Industry

This faculty aims to nurture engineers who can resolve various issues facing modern civilization from a technological standpoint and contribute to the creation of new industries of the future.

HAPPY SCIENCE ACADEMY
JUNIOR AND SENIOR HIGH SCHOOL

Happy Science Academy Junior and Senior High School is a boarding school founded with the goal of educating the future leaders of the world who can have a big vision, persevere, and take on new challenges. Currently, there are two campuses in Japan; the Nasu Main Campus in Tochigi Prefecture, founded in 2010, and the Kansai Campus in Shiga Prefecture, founded in 2013.

ABOUT IRH PRESS USA

IRH Press USA Inc. was founded in 2013 as an affiliated firm of IRH Press Co., Ltd. Based in New York, the press publishes books in various categories including spirituality, religion, and self-improvement and publishes books by Ryuho Okawa, the author of 100 million books sold worldwide. For more information, visit OkawaBooks.com.

Follow us on:
Facebook: Okawa Books
Twitter: Okawa Books
Goodreads: Ryuho Okawa
Instagram: OkawaBooks
Pinterest: Okawa Books

RYUHO OKAWA'S LAWS SERIES

The Laws Series is an annual volume of books that are mainly comprised of Ryuho Okawa's lectures on various topics that highlight principles and guidelines for the activities of Happy Science every year. *The Laws of the Sun*, the first publication of the laws series, ranked in the annual best-selling list in Japan in 1994. Since then, all of the laws series' titles have ranked in the annual best-selling list for more than two decades, setting socio-cultural trends in Japan and around the world.

THE TRILOGY

The first three volumes of the Laws Series, *The Laws of the Sun*, *The Golden Laws*, and *The Nine Dimensions* make a trilogy that completes the basic framework of the teachings of God's Truths. *The Laws of the Sun* discusses the structure of God's Laws, *The Golden Laws* expounds on the doctrine of time, and *The Nine Dimensions* reveals the nature of space.

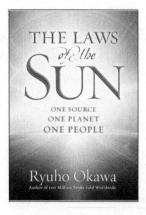

THE LAWS OF THE SUN
One Source, One Planet, One People

Hardcover • 264 pages • $24.95
• ISBN: 978-1-937673-04-8

Imagine if you could ask God why he created this world and what spiritual laws he used to shape us—and everything around us. In *The Laws of the Sun*, Okawa outlines these laws of the universe and provides a road map for living one's life with greater purpose and meaning. This powerful book shows the way to realize true happiness—a happiness that continues from this world through the other.

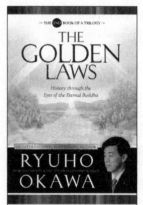

THE GOLDEN LAWS

History through the Eyes of the Eternal Buddha

Softcover • 216 pages • $14.95
• ISBN: 978-1-941779-81-1

Throughout history, Great Guiding Spirits of Light have been present on Earth in both the East and the West at crucial points in human history to further our spiritual development. Among them were Shakyamuni Buddha, Jesus Christ, Confucius, Socrates, Krishna, and Mohammed. *The Golden Laws* reveals how Divine Plan has been unfolding on Earth, and outlines 5,000 years of the secret history of humankind. Once we understand the true course of history, through past, present and into the future, we cannot help but become aware of the significance of our spiritual mission in the present age.

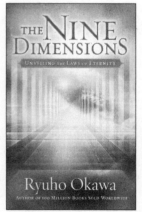

THE NINE DIMENSIONS

Unveiling the Laws of Eternity

Softcover • 168 pages • $15.95
• ISBN: 978-0-982698-56-3

This book is a window into the mind of our loving God, who designed this world and the vast, wondrous world of our afterlife as a school with many levels through which our souls learn and grow. When the religions and cultures of the world discover the truth of their common spiritual origin, they will be inspired to accept their differences, come together under faith in God, and build an era of harmony and peaceful progress on Earth.

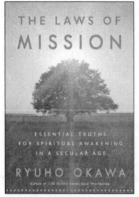

THE LAWS OF MISSION

Essential Truths for Spiritual Awakening
in a Secular Age

Softcover • 224 pages • $15.95
• ISBN: 978-1-942125-24-2

This book shows how we can discover and unleash
the power of our mind to create a better future,
how we can find faith and awaken to our purpose
in this world, and how we can create a world of
happiness by spreading the spiritual truths around
the world. Okawa's empowering and inspiring
messages will bring about spiritual, religious, academic, political, and economic breakthroughs
in the world that has increasingly become more
secular.

THE LAWS OF SUCCESS

A Spiritual Guide to Turning
Your Hopes Into Reality

Softcover • 208 pages • $15.95
• ISBN: 978-1-942125-15-0

The Laws of Success offers 8 spiritual principles
that, when put to practice in our day-to-day
life, will help us attain lasting success and let us
experience the fulfillment of living our purpose
and the joy of sharing our happiness with many
others. The timeless wisdom and practical steps
that Okawa offers will guide us through any difficulties and problems we may face in life, and
serve as guiding principles for living a positive,
constructive, and meaningful life.

THE LAWS OF JUSTICE
How We Can Solve World Conflicts and Bring Peace

Softcover • 208 pages • $15.95
• ISBN: 978-1-942125-05-1

This book shows what global justice is from a comprehensive perspective of the Supreme God. Becoming aware of this view will let us embrace differences in beliefs, recognize other peoples divine nature, and love and forgive one another. It will also become the key to solving the issues we face, whether they are religious, political, societal, economic, or academic, and help the world become a better and safer world for all of us living today.

LIST OF OTHER BOOKS BY RYUHO OKAWA

THE STARTING POINT OF HAPPINESS
An Inspiring Guide to Positive Living with Faith, Love, and Courage

INVINCIBLE THINKING
An Essential Guide for a Lifetime of Growth, Success, and Triumph

HEALING FROM WITHIN
Life-Changing Keys to Calm, Spiritual, and Healthy Living

THE UNHAPPINESS SYNDROME
28 Habits of Unhappy People (and How to Change Them)

A LIFE OF TRIUMPH
Unleashing Your Light Upon the World

THE MIRACLE OF MEDITATION
Opening Your Life to Peace, Joy, and the Power Within

THE HEART OF WORK
10 Keys to Living Your Calling

THE ESSENCE OF BUDDHA
The Path to Enlightenment

THINK BIG!
Be Positive and Be Brave to Achieve Your Dreams

INVITATION TO HAPPINESS
7 Inspirations from Your Inner Angel

MESSAGES FROM HEAVEN
What Jesus, Buddha, Muhammad, and Moses Would Say Today

SECRETS OF THE EVERLASTING TRUTHS
A New Paradigm for Living on Earth

THE MOMENT OF TRUTH
Become a Living Angel Today

CHANGE YOUR LIFE, CHANGE THE WORLD
A Spiritual Guide to Living Now

For a complete list of books, visit OkawaBooks.com.